AMERICAN CRYPTIDS

In Pursuit of the Elusive Creatures

KENNEY W. IRISH

BEYOND THE FRAY

Publishing

ISBN 13: 978-1-954528-01-7

First edition: 2020 / Second edition: 2021

Beyond The Fray Publishing, a division of Beyond The Fray, LLC, San
Diego, CA
www.beyondthefraypublishing.com

To my beautiful daughter, Hailey Belle

Acknowledgments

Thank you first to God.

Thank you to my best friend and wife, Selena Denise.

I would also like to thank these folks who have supported in ways from just an encouraging word, to other acts of support (in no particular order) All Dark Moon Press authors, Michael Massey, Denis & Martha Chevalier, Chris Tebbetts, Ken Gerhard, Angel Vaow, E.R. Vernor, Wayne Lavitt, Brian Dorn, Gary Robusto, Luke Pullen, Leighann Thorsey, Joe Anzovino, Michael Donahue, Isabel Prescott & family, Karen Sturtevant, Shaun Stotyn, Jennifer Hale, Jason Miller, Edward Monge, C. Wayne Totherow, Andrea Anesi, Emily Menshouse, Jason Hoyt, Ted Van Son, Todd Campbell, Allie Daigle, Deniel Benoit, Katy Elizabeth, Ron Yacovetti, Kevin Maxwell, Ramey Armell, Ashley Storm, Dan Olson.

I would like to thank these organizations (in no particular order) Dark Moon Press, Culligan by WaterCo, New York Bigfoot Society, Tri-City NY Paranormal, Bigfoot Quest Radio, The Rochester Winter Para-feast, Mannimal Research, Paratalk Radio, We Are Paradox Media, Coast to Coast AM with George Noory, W.T. Frick Live, Beacon of Light Radio

Show, Storming the Unknown Podcast, Paravation at the Strasburg Historical, Darknite Radio, Portland Maine Paracon, Champ Day-The Lake Champlain Monster Festival, International Bigfoot Conference, NYS Writers Institute, Bear Pond Books, Fright Fest, Bigfoot the Real Truth, Cryptovania, Sasquatch Festival Whitehall New York, Musser Lake Bigfoot Research Center, CORRIDOR13

Introduction

Ken Gerhard

"If I cannot inspire love, I will cause fear." So famously pronounced the creature in Mary Shelley's classic, Gothic horror novel Frankenstein. Shelley's tragic monster represented the quintessential cherub – combining both grotesque features, as well as a baneful innocence.

Yet, are all of our monsters merely constructs of fable and fiction? Not if we are to believe the far-reaching tales that portray humongous, shaggy, manlike monsters stalking the outer reaches of modern America. Moreover, there is a wealth of other evidence – startling in its conformity and generally unfamiliar to the average person – that points to the existence of, a race of sub-human giants who exist, just beyond the grasp of scientific acceptance.

Throughout the years, I've been unquestionably blessed to have had an opportunity to travel all across this awe-inspiring North American continent – from the remote, snow-covered peaks of Alaska to the impenetrable marshes of Florida – often times on the trail of incomprehensible monsters. And while some so-called "cryptids" seem to be sensational composites that combine misinterpretations of known animals with tall tales and wishful thinking – this most definitely is not the case with regard to the Sasquatch, more commonly referred to as – Bigfoot.

For the unconvinced, I like to break the evidence down into layers. First, we must look back – way back in time to the geological period known as the Pleistocene epoch, beginning over two million years ago. During that stage, smaller versions of Bigfoot actually did exist on the continent of Africa. We have definitive proof of this in the form of their fossilized bones. Known as the robust australopithecines, these veritable "ape-men" were a mosaic of both – hair-covered and power-ful, but walking very much like us, upright and on two legs. It is not hard to imagine how these ancient hominids may have radiated out of Africa at some point, spreading into Asia. Perhaps then crossing the land bridge that once existed between the Old World and North America. During the Ice Age, these beings may have gotten even hairier and grown to immense sizes – similar to the woolly rhinos and mammoths of that frozen era.

These theoretical man-beasts would have co-existed with Native Americans for the past 12,000 years and lo, there are in fact numerous, centuries-old, native traditions, which describe a gigantic, hairy tribe who choose to dwell deep in the wilder-ness. Then there are the modern reports – thousands of them, consistently describing encounters with the monster we call Bigfoot. I've personally interviewed hundreds of eyewitnesses, many of them impressive and sincere in their convictions that they have come across a creature that science tells us should not exist. One controversial film that was captured at Bluff Creek, California during 1967, seems to show one of these monsters striding away into the forest. Skeptics continually argue that the subject is merely a man wearing a costume, but conveniently ignore the fact that realistic costumes did not exist at the time. And finally, we have the footprints, thousands of them, usually found in places where man seldom goes; superficially humanlike, but much too large and bearing features that some experts have conceded are irrefutable proof that a living, breathing, giant walks among us.

Within the following pages, you will discover some fifty testimonials that attest to this startling reality – that Bigfoot may be found somewhere in every one of the United States. Fortunately, researcher and author Kenney W. Irish is in a prime position to relate these fascinating and often chilling accounts. An experienced Bigfoot investigator living in upstate New York, Kenney has had a lifelong interest in many facets of the unexplained – from UFO reports, to the paranormal, to all manner of strange cryptids and monsters – and he's spent a considerable amount of time looking into these enduring mysteries. Irish is particularly intrigued by how our perception of these varied phenomena are colored by folkloric influences. As a bonus, the author offers a titillating taste of local culture – relating meaningful facts about each state's history and heritage. In many respects, I could not be more delighted to introduce this very enjoyable, Bigfoot travelogue and I am exceedingly confident that the curious reader will agree!

Ken Gerhard – San Antonio, TX

Foreword
Katy Elizabeth

Bigfoot or Sasquatch are said to be hairy, upright-walking, ape-like creatures that dwell in the wilderness. Depictions often portray them as a missing link between humans, human ancestors, or other great apes. They are strongly associated with the Pacific Northwest. On the other hand, these creatures have been reported throughout the United States. With around four hundred sightings reported each year, these creatures have maintained their elusive nature, and have continued as a scientific enigma.

Combined, the Native American tribes of North America, have more than sixty different names for Sasquatch. Are the native legends of these hairy beasts just myth? Native Americans were not the only people seeing this hairy, primate creature, roaming the wilderness of America. Nineteenth- and early 20th-century newspapers, had whole sections devoted to the miners, trappers, gold prospectors, and woodsmen claiming to have seen, "wildmen," "bear men," and "monkey men."

Most famously, in 1924, a group of prospectors hunkering down in a cabin along the shoulder of Mount St. Helen in Washington State, claimed they were attacked late one night by a group of "ape-men." Later, one of the prospectors admitted that they were not unprovoked attacks. He had taken potshots at the creatures earlier that day.

Experts estimate that there are around 2,000-6,000 Sasquatch within the United States and Canada. Kenney W. Irish presents, not only an extensive, but impressive collection of compiled eyewitness reports from across the country. This material is a must read. An intriguing look into these bi-pedal beasts known collectively as, Bigfoot.

Katy Elizabeth - Vermont

Katy Elizabeth was born in Warwick Rhode Island. Katy is a world-leading authority on the Lake Champlain Monster. She has been studying the existence of Champ since a child. She made her lifelong dream into reality when she had her own sighting, and experiences of this elusive creature in Lake Champlain. This prompted her to start her own group called, "Champ Search." The group's goal is to study, investigate, prove the existence, and most importantly, protect the unique animals that inhabit New York and Vermont's beautiful Lake Champlain. Katy currently resides on the shores of Lake Champlain in VT.

In 2018, she was honored with an official world record, as the only full-time Dedicated Woman Lake Monster Hunter in the world. Also, in 2018, Katy approached the town of Port Henry NY, known as the "Home of Champ," with a written resolution to protect these creatures. April of 2018, this law was passed. Katy has been featured on the History Channel, Discovery Channel, The Science Channel, NBC, and Coast to Coast AM. She is the author of the new book, *Water Horse of Lake Champlain: The Search.*

1

Evidence

WHAT EXACTLY IS CONSIDERED EVIDENCE? Is it the
unidentified howl in the dead of night? A lurking figure in the
woods for no reason? Could it be a footprint that just could not
be human? Maybe a picture of something that should not be.
Regardless of what "evidence" is presented, it is always open
for opinion and scrutiny. Some have created a false reality of
who and what these creatures are and represent. Made out to
be fun and in most cases laughable, anyone who comes across
one's path certainly does not walk away smiling, but always in a
state of shock.

Unfortunately, some distorted and weakened the perspec-
tive and understanding of the individuals who relentlessly
pursue these beings looking for answers. From Native American folklore dating back hundreds of years, to present day
monster encounters. In the end, when looking past the lights of
fame and scripted entertainment, there is one aspect that
remains, cannot be denied, nor overlooked. The countless
witnesses across the United States who claim encounters with
what can only be described as, American Cryptids.

The Native Americans have long played a role in the documentation of sightings regarding what we now call Sasquatch or Bigfoot. Some tribes referred to the creature as "Wildman" due to its human like bi-pedal walk. I also give credit of knowledge to the Indigenous People when it comes to other mysterious and unexplained creatures. With so many tribes, I cannot mention all, but will be highlighting some historical information about one in each chapter from each state.

I have been researching and studying legend and lore my entire life. My mind which I refer to as my "internal hard-drive," has been overflowing with the stories and legends. So, now it is time to download the information into this publication.

On average, depending on what data one pursues, in the United States there are about four hundred sightings reported each year. Of these eyewitness encounters, most want to stay anonymous due to the fear of backlash and ridicule. As promised, written records containing any direct information has been destroyed in an effort, to respect the privacy of each. Thanks to word of mouth and modern-day technology, contacting and obtaining encounters from each state has not been such the task I first believed it to be.

Cleburne County, AL
STATE PARK DWELLER

ALABAMA NICKNAMED, THE "HEART OF DIXIE," is a southeastern US state and displays many landmarks that represent the American Civil Rights Movement. Its capital is Montgomery. Alabama joined the union as the 22nd state in 1819. In the mid-20th century, Alabama was at the center of the American Civil Rights Movement and was also part of the Montgomery Bus Boycott. The state's economy was energized in the twenty-first century with employment in areas such as agriculture, auto production, and jobs in the aerospace industry. Its population is approximately five million, with an area covering 52,420 squares miles.

Alabama is home to tribes of Cherokee Native Americans. The population of Native Americans significantly contributed to shaping the state's history. The Cherokees contributed and served as valuable allies to the United States at the time of the Creek War from 1813 to 1814. When war presented itself in 1813, the Cherokees fought alongside US troops under Andrew Jackson. As one, they raided Creek villages along the Black Warrior River and fought in the 1813 battles of

Tallushatchee and Talladega from which they emerged victorious. The Cherokee believed in the Thunder Beings. It is said they live in rainbows and lightning. It is also believed that the Thunders who lived close to the earth's surface would harm the people which did happen from time to time.

Alabama is also home to The Wampus Cat, a panther sized beast with glowing yellow eyes. Some claim the eyes could pierce a man's soul, or even launch an individual into a trans-like state, unable to move or defend themselves. Witness encounters claim the legend as a cross between a beast like feline creature, and a woman. Some have witness canine dog-like features as well. The howl is said to evoke anxiety and fear upon whoever experiences the vocal. The lucky individuals who have encountered and lived to tell the tale, have claimed the beast, while mostly on all fours as you would expect, has the unnatural ability to walk bipedal and give chase on just the two hind-legs.

The Cherokee Tribe believe the beast to be of spirit, yet can transform itself into a flesh-like human form, to lure in unsuspecting victims. The beast is said to be nocturnal in nature, which adds an advantage when hunting for human prey. Some poor souls have been taken in the night while they slept. The folklore surrounding the Wampus Cat has been passed down through generations, and across native tribes. Stating the evil that lurks the land is in fact real, and directs and heaths warning to all not to venture away on your own, and to always keep one eye open.

THE "STATE PARK DWELLER," a large bi-pedal creature witnessed many times in Cleburne County. Eyewitnesses have claimed that the Dweller stands seven to eight-feet-tall with a shoulder-to-shoulder width of four-feet. Its fur has been described as knotted and of "light color." Some believe it is an offspring to the most popular Bigfoot known in Alabama as the "White Thang" but at this point it is a theory that cannot be validated. From what can be confirmed thus far, the creature received its name from being seen mostly at night in state parks around the area. Some witnesses have claimed that the Dweller was going through dumpsters looking for food and being seen ravaging through coolers at campsites. Black bears are known to have been seen in the area, but according to campers, these encounters all can be "confirmed" as not a bear, as the creature they witnessed was of a light color which aligns with the Dwellers description.

One encounter took place on a Friday night approximately around 10:30 p.m. A couple who was staying at the Cleburne State Park took a stroll on what they described as a path that seemed to be more like a wildlife trail traveled by forest animals in the area. As they walked, they could only describe their surroundings as peaceful and serene. The moon glared through the tree's which cast enough light to help guide them along. Out of nowhere they came across a foul smell. Thinking it was possibly just a dead animal somewhere they continued. The smell worsened to the point they decided to turn back as they felt that they would be coming across whatever it was if they continued forward.

As they turned around, and started back toward the direction of the park, just to the right was a large tree and there appeared to be a large figure standing behind it peering out at them. They described the figure to have yellow glowing eyes. The height of where the eyes sat would have been around the eight-foot mark according to the couple. The creature made no noise but seemed to be swaying back and forth. The pair took off running, when they arrived back at their site, packed up all their belongings and left. The encounter has been etched in their minds and at this point, they will no longer consider camping in a state park again.

Gateway County, AK
WHIPPLE CREEK SCREAMER

ALASKA, called by some "Land of the Midnight sun" whose capital is Juneau, was acquired by the United States in 1867 for $7.2 million which was approved by the US Congress, and the American flag was flown at Sitka. It was the 49th state to join the union. Gold was discovered on the Stikine River in 1861 and in Juneau in 1880. In 1878 a salmon cannery was constructed which was the beginning of what became the largest salmon industry in the world.

In the 1950s, oil and natural gas discoveries in the Kenai Peninsula and offshore drilling in Cook inlet, created an industry that by the mid 1970s, ranked first in the states mineral production. In the 1960s a booming pulp industry began to utilize the forest resources. Today, the population is approximately over seven-hundred-thousand with an area covering 664,988 square miles. It is documented that in 1971, the temperature dropped to a record low of -80 degrees.

Alaska is also home to the Yupik Tribe. The Yupik group of Indians known as Eskimos and is closely related to the Inupiat and Inuit Alaskan Tribes. These great people are the reason the Kayak is in existence. A big part of their survival is related to hunting. A Yupik diet consists of salmon, seal, and whales. Today the population is approximately over twenty-two-thousand and they still practice their traditional hunting practices. They live out the Shaman religion which believes that you can achieve various powers through trance, or ecstatic experience. The Yupik also have a custom of naming their newborn children after the last person who died in the community. The Yupik people can also be found residing in Russia and other locations outside of Alaska. The tribe feared the "A-mi'-kuk." This was a creature that was described as very large with leathery type skin that was at times slimy. It was said to grab its victims with its tentacle type arms and pull them to the depths of the water. Many who had disappeared were believed to have fallen victim to this creature.

WHEN IN ALASKA, you will certainly hear of the legend surrounding the Kodiak Dinosaur. It has been said, due to the enormous size of the creature, the first eyewitnesses in 1969 dubbed it a "dinosaur." The first press to cover the story and discovery of this such beast, was the Kodiak Mirror Press. The publications story revolves around an Alaskan shrimping boat that was equipped with state-of-the-art surveillance equipment, using sonar technology. The sonar images of the lurking creature in the deep sea, claim measurements from one-hundred and fifty to two-hundred-feet in length. The image also revealed the creature to having a long thin neck, with a serpentine shaped head. The middle area surrounding the body according to the image, was thick with flipper-like arms protruding from the right and left side, of what was considered to be the sides of the creature. The aquatic beast, to some is just a hoax, or just simply faulty equipment. Either way, according to many recent encounters, the Kodiak Dinosaur is said to be as real as the "Loch Ness Monster," and "Ogopogo."

⊏⊐

THERE IS another being who calls Alaska its home. Known for its hideous screams, it has been dubbed "The Whipple Creek Screamer" by the residents in the area. Descriptions of the creature vary from seven to nine-feet-tall. It has been described as having dark brown to black colored fur with red glowing eyes. Some have claimed the creature may have breasts leaning toward it being female.

A strange claim from residents says for some reason it has an extra interest in folks who live in trailers. The one aspect of the Whipple Creek Screamer that never changes or can be denied is the scream it bellows. It has been described as sounding like a woman giving birth or in excruciating pain. The unlucky people who have been close enough to hear it, claim that once you experience it, you can never unhear it. It just sticks with you each day. You hope and pray that you make it through the night without experiencing its intense power and spine tingling vocal.

One unlucky man in the early 2000s had an experience with the creature. Under the worst of circumstances this encounter took place. While at home one night there was a power outage in the area. The trailer the man lived in went pitch dark. This is not an uncommon occurrence in the area, so he was not overly concerned. Having a backup generator outside he quickly put on his jacket, grabbed a flashlight, a pistol then ventured out into the cold. He went to the side of the trailer where the generator was housed in a makeshift container to protect it from the elements. The man claimed he struggled with removing the lock which was frozen. In his upset and enraged state, he yelled out some obscenities. Much to his surprise, about five-seconds after, there was a scream that seem to come from what he described as about fifty-yards away in a thick area of forest.

This reply to his initial yelling was unwelcome. As he turned around, he pointed the flashlight in the direction of the noise and witnessed a large figure standing in the distance. Facial features could not be made out, but according to the surrounding frozen vegetation the figure seemed to measure up into the eight-foot realm. It let out another scream and the effects of the scream could be felt hitting the man's chest. He raised his pistol, took a shot. Unsure if he hit the figure, it let out another scream and ran off into the thicket. The man quickly retreated inside and allegedly called the authorities. There was evidence of something in the area where the man saw the figure lurking, but it could not be determined what it was. As far as the bullet hitting the figure, there was no blood or evidence of a hit. The encounter was played off as being a "bear" sighting which was a common occurrence in the area. The man was warned by the authorities to be sure in the future what he was pointing the pistol at before pulling the trigger.

4

Gila County, AZ
NINE-FOOT-TALL FISHERMAN

ARIZONA, which was originally part of Mexico achieved state-hood in 1912 as the 48th state to join the union. The land was ceded to the United States in 1848 and became a separate territory in the year 1863. In 1854, copper was discovered, and mining became Arizona's primary type of industry up until the 1950s. Another interesting fact, Arizona's population began to increase due in part of the availability of air conditioning. Due to this it became one of the fastest growing states in America. The population is approximately over 6 million and is the 6th largest state in the country regarding area. The size comes in at 113,990 square miles.

Arizona is also home to the Apache Indian tribe. The Apache have a rich prosperous history in the area. Having many struggles, they always overcame. Apache men were trained for combat war at a very young age. They are hunters, warriors and some have become political leaders. The men wore leather war shirts and breechcloths in the warm weather. When temperatures would drop, they were known to wear buffalo skin for warmth. The Apache women wore cloths made of buckskin. They always had long hair and would decorate with handmade ornaments. The women wore warrior shirts which were often decorated with beads. The main source of food for the Apache tribes would consist of buffalo, but also consumed turkey, fox, elk, and deer. The Apache believed and feared what they called the Big Owl or the "La-Lechuza." The people would blame this being for unusual deaths and unexplained events. The Big Owl was referred to when it came to the children as the Boogeyman.

THE STATE of Arizona has many legends of lore, surprisingly some surrounding werewolves. The werewolf, some say to be half-man, and half wolf. Others claim the being to be a cursed man that transforms into a wolf when a full moon occurs. The legend of the werewolf has been in existence throughout history, and stories of encounters with such beasts have been passed down from generation to generation. During the times of witch trials, they also held werewolf trials. Many folks who were considered to be a werewolf and found guilty, were burned to death. For most, a wolfman type creature is seen as the 1941 "Hollywood" character, whose death comes via a silver bullet. But there are countless real-life accounts that have been recorded over the centuries.

Many unexplained mutilated "human" deaths are said to be the work of a werewolf. Vision of the remains are said to have long deep claw marks down the back, which leads many to believe there was a foot chase, and the front having the stomach and chest area ripped open and pulled apart. These such findings are almost always written off as some kind of "fierce" animal attack. Werewolves are also suspect when it comes to farm animal mutilation and missing livestock. One eyewitness, a farmer claimed he heard a commotion near his hen house. He grabbed his rifle and ran outside. He came across a man-like creature with canine features that stood up while dropping the dead hen on the ground. The farmer took a shot at the beast. Once the rifle went off, it fled into the darkness. This encounter left the farmer shaken, and now uncomfortable on his own property.

———

IN THE ROOSEVELT Lake area in Gila County, there is a beast known to two men as the nine-foot-tall Fisherman. Described as having unusually thin legs with a large flat nose. The eyes have been detailed as glowing red and the body with dark brown hair. Like many other Sasquatches, it has been said that it puts off a retched odor that once experienced, it will never be forgotten.

Two gentlemen were fishing in the early morning hours in the area of Roosevelt Lake. It is an area they were both familiar with as it was a common location, they would frequently fish. As they made their way along the lake, they noticed an odor that was described as "hot garbage and rotting fish." Being by the lake and wildlife in the area, it was assumed that it was a rotting carcass of some poor animal that fell prey to another.

One of the men noticed movement from the corner of his eye. He turned in the direction and stopped dead in his tracks. The man's friend turned, looked, and witnessed the same sight his friend was focused on. The creature was about seventy-five-yards away, looked to be in the nine-foot range. It took huge strides while walking and swinging its arm. The hair was dark brown, but the creature was not close enough to see any type of texture to it. They just stood silent and watched it as it disappeared into a line of trees. Since that day, the two fishermen have had many conversations about that early morning encounter going over the "maybe it was this, or maybe it was that" scenarios. But to this day, they just do not believe there was a nine-foot fisherman they were witnessing that morning.

5

Benton County, AR
APE LIKE MAN

ARKANSAS, whose capital is Little Rock, has a statehood date of 1836 and was the 25th state to join the union. The present-day Arkansas ranks 27th among the fifty states in area at 53,178 square miles. In 1957, Little Rock Central High School attracted national attention when it sent troops to the school to support integration. Today the population is approximately three million.

The Osaga Indians hunted and claimed the northwestern area which included all land as far south as the Arkansas River. The men hunted elk, bison, deer, and bear. The women would butcher the animals, smoke the meat, and prepare the hides. The men wore deerskin loincloths, leggings with moccasins. When it was colder outside, they would wear bearskin robes. The women kept their hair long and wore deerskin dresses, leggings with moccasins. In 1808, they ceded most of the land to the United States Government in a treaty that was signed off in Fork Clark, in Louisiana territory. The Osaga people believed in what they called the Wild People. A fairy-like little people that would roam the forests and were blamed for many unexplained events and rare occurrences.

IF YOU EVER VISITED ARKANSAS, I have no doubt you will hear tales of the Ozark Howler. Described by some, as a bear sized dog with sharp goat-like horns protruding out of each side of its head. Its body is said to be covered in long dark matted hair, and resembles a bear's torso. On the backside it displays a long-jagged tail that can be used in a type of defense, swinging at its victims. It has human-like hands with large type claws that are said to be able to extend out and retract. Its hind legs and feet mimic a large wolf. The Howlers eyes are described as bright glowing red. This occurs naturally as if the eyes are engulfed in flames. The howl is distinct in vocal range, and can be heard from miles away. Its described as sounding wolf-like, but with a low guttural bear growl at the end. Some have even claimed and believe that it is part human, due to hearing its scream, as it resembles a human crying out in terror. The Native Americans have spoken of the Howler since the 1800s. Some lore claims the creature could scale up the side of a tree, where it would sit and await its next victim. Upon identifying the prey, whether it to be human or animal, it would then pounce, mutilate and devour. Arkansas residents, beware, and always be looking up.

ANOTHER CREATURE that certainly roams the state but less talked about is known as the "Ape Like Creature." Given its name since it looks like a large ape but standing over seven-feet-tall, it falls under the Sasquatch category. Mostly witnessed in Benton County, some originally thought it was an ape on the loose. That certainly was not the case.

Two men who unexpectedly came face to face with this creature in a secluded area were reported to be so shaken up that medical treatment was needed. They would not give details. In 2009 some young men gathered in the deep woods to have a relaxing night sitting by a fire. Some beers were consumed, but according to them not enough to impair their judgment or vision. The claims are a Bigfoot entered their camp and violently started tearing the tents down. Scaring the young men, they retreated but not before a shot was fired at the creature. One of the gathering attendees was hurdled through the air into a tree. The young men allegedly notified the authorities and described the creature as a "large ape." The young men's report according to them, was dismissed as a "mis-identification" and went nowhere.

6

Del Norte County, CA
ROADSIDE LEAPER

CALIFORNIA, whose capital is Sacramento became a US Territory in 1847 as part of the treaty that ended the Mexican American war. In 1848 gold was discovered at Sutters Mill which set a wave of new settlers to the West coast in hopes of being the ones to find a fortune. In 1850, California became the 31st state to join the union and is now the 3rd largest in the USIn agriculture, California leads the way in production. The state is home to Hollywood, the Golden Gate Bridge, Yosemite National Park and Disneyland. Its population is well over thirty-seven million and it is 163,694 square miles.

Today the Tolowa Dee-ni' are a federally recognized Indian Nation. The homeland, the Taa-laa-waa-dvn can be found along the pacific northwest coast. The traditional home was constructed in a rectangular single ridged roof structure. It was usually built into the ground using planks, pine timbers and cedar wood. The Tolowa's diet would consist of salmon, whale, elk, deer and seal for protein and acorns with vegetables for carbohydrates. The tribe believed in and feared what they called the Thunder Bird. The creature was described as a large reptile bird with a large sharp beak and a bald head. It is said that it would swoop down on unsuspecting folks and carry them away to devour.

———

THE STATE of California is well known for the Bob Gimlin and Roger Patterson film, of the famous Bigfoot known as "Patty." Still today it has not been debunked, although many have tried. The footage was shot on 16mm film. Both men had become intrigued with the possibility of a creature existing, and set out on an attempt to capture a Sasquatch on film. On horseback, Bob and Roger set out with a rented camera in hopes of gaining footage of the elusive creature. The trip was planned to be for a couple of weeks across rough terrain and many miles. In the early afternoon hours on October 20, 1967, the two men would come across what they had set out to accomplish and change the world of Bigfoot as we knew it. The Bigfoot who was dubbed "Patty," walked out into a clearing which allowed the two men to film what is considered today, to be the gold standard of Sasquatch videos.

It is believed that the creature was female, as the image in the video appears to have breasts. The creature walks through the open area, looks back just for a moment, then disappears deep in the forest. Bob and Roger also came across footprints that they made plaster casts out of. The two men then rode back to Willow Creek. They sent the age off to be developed, and once it was ready and arrived, it was presented to the world. To this day it still holds up its validity over all other presented Sasquatch videos.

———

ANOTHER, but not so famous creature from the state that has been described as having brown fur, a horrible smell and stands in the seven and half foot range. Known to some as the "Road-side Leaper" as it seems to have more of a jump and leap than an actual walk. This could be due in part to injury, but at this point that is just a theory. Most encounters seem to take place late at night or the early morning hours in the form of a road crossing. Unlike most Sasquatch sightings, the witnesses seem to get a better look at the Roadside Leaper due to its inability to run. When dash cams and eyewitnesses encounter a road crossing it is very quick and brief.

In the spring of 2006 near the Patrick Creek Campground, a gentleman was traveling on US Route 199 on his way to an appointment. The road was clear with only another passing vehicle once every ten-minutes or so. While coming around a bend in the road, another car sped by flashing their lights. Thinking there could be a possible police officer ahead he checked his speed and according to his speedometer he was well in the legal limit he should be. As he looked up, a huge figure on the side of the road seem to step out with a sort of jump leap. The surprised man hit the brakes with the wheels screeching. The figure then turned back and retreated into the nearby woods. It seemed to leap and jump. The man was distraught at what he had seen. To this day, the man has never seen the creature again or anything like it. He still to this day travels down that same road quite often. Every time he comes to that same bend in the road, anxiety overtakes him, his stomach starts to ache and his head pounds. Once past the encounter location, he can calm himself down. But he will never be the same again.

7

Park County, CO
ROCK MOUNTAIN MONSTER

COLORADO, whose capital is Denver joined the statehood in 1876 and is America's 8th largest state in land mass. It was the 38th state to join the union. It is 104,094 square miles with an approximate population of over five million. Colorado is in the Rocky Mountain region of the Western United States. In 1858, gold was discovered which increased the number of settlers coming into the area. An interesting fact about Colorado: it is the only state to ever reject hosting the Winter Olympics in 1976 as the voters were against using tax state revenue to help finance the event.

The Arapaho Indians have lived in the Colorado plains since the seventeenth century. They refer to themselves as 'Inuna-Ina' which mean's "our people." The Arapaho lived in teepees made from hunted buffalo skins. The teepees were easily set up and taken down which was ideal when having to move from location to location. As expert buffalo hunters, the buffalo can provide the tribe with all they need for shelter, clothing, and nutrition. They are also known to hunt deer and elk and consume plants and wild berries. The Arapaho are spiritual people, who believe in an overall creator who they refer to as "Be He Teiht." The people also believed and fear what they referred to as the Cannibal Dwarves. They are described as child size and having a thirst for human blood. It is said that they were fierce when it came too fighting and could run an adult male down and feast.

———

DO YOU BELIEVE IN VAMPIRES? The folks of Colorado certainly do. According to history, in the 1800s vampires made their way into the state and still today, folks speak of frightening sightings and encounters. When one thinks of vampires, in most cases the image of the infamous "Dracula" is what's envisioned. Living in a large dark castle, a tall individual with slicked back hair, very well dressed, wearing a long black cape, having pale skin and fangs. With a lusting thirst for human blood, it is believed Dracula who is nocturnal, transforms into a bat and ventures off into the night in search of a suitable victim. In most cases, he hunts down and stalks women, biting the curve of their neck and consuming their blood. After the feeding he returns to his place of rest. A casket, to avoid sunlight that will in fact kill him if exposed. A wooden stake to the heart is also considered to be deadly to him.

However, real-life vampires do not follow all of Hollywood's original narrative or version. They come in all body forms and can be both male and female. They dress in most part as anyone would depending on their style or taste. However, most are pale skinned but can absorb sunlight without concern of death. All do in fact have a thirst for human blood. They have the ability to appear and disappear, which makes a human victim easy prey. Once they have subdued the victim, either physically, or in some cases staring into the eyes of the individual putting them into an unconscious trance. They then indulge in the body fluids, draining away the life and soul of the unfortunate individual. It is said, that if the victim survives the attack but has been bitten, they will themselves, become a vampire. For those who escape the grasp of a vampire, without a bite and live to tell the tale, are never the same again. I cannot confirm this claim, but many say that the person eventually goes insane and is admitted to an institution. Others disappear, and it is believed that the original vampire had returned to finish the attack.

⸻

ANOTHER BEING that seems to have folks on their toes is a large, five-hundred-pound, eight-and-half foot-tall, brown in color, Sasquatch known to some as the "Rock Mountain Monster." Named after its existence in the Rocky Mountain area of Colorado, this creature is known to throw rocks at unsuspecting hikers, campers and anyone who gets too close to what the creature feels is "their" territory. The territory could be in the mountains or along a roadway.

In 2002 a couple were hiking and exploring in Park County in the Camp Santa Maria area. As they strolled near the North Fork of the South Platte River, they experienced a musty like garbage smell. Assuming there was a corpse of an unlucky animal, they continued. As they came to this one area of the river, they noticed what appeared to be large footprints. They jokingly laughed at the fact they both though of the legend Bigfoot, which neither believed in. Out of nowhere a rock went buzzing by the woman's head almost hitting her. The man yelled in the direction it came from for the person to come out, which was a somewhat thick area of trees. There was no vocal reply, but the man's request was answered with another big stone that hit the ground next to him, leaving a deep gash in the ground and bounced a few times before it stopped at its final resting point. They could not see anyone but due to the size of the last stone that was thrown, they took off running in the opposite direction fearing for their lives. The fear of whatever was throwing the stones chasing them kept them from looking back. The couple through the whole ordeal never saw anyone or anything. They will not say for a fact that it was a Sasquatch. With that said, they do believe that after this encounter with whatever it was, it's an experience they will never forget or ever want to go through again.

8

Hartford County, CT
RIVER MYSTERY

CONNECTICUT, which is in the northeastern area of the country, calls its capital Hartford. It celebrates its statehood that occurred in 1788 and was the 5th state to join the union. It is one of the thirteen colonies and one of the six New England states. Machine manufacturing and textile was where the state dominated and made its mark in the industry. Connecticut was also a leading manufacturer of guns and other arms. The state ranks as the 3rd smallest at 5,544 square miles but has a large population at just under four million.

When we think of Connecticut and locations to visit, the Mohegan Sun casino in Uncasville is always a place of interest. Run by the Mohegan tribe, they have a long rich history in the state. The Mohegan tribe like many others, had specific roles for men and women. The men were hunters and at times went to war to protect the tribe and families. The women had more of a farmer type role along with the cooking and childcare. The tribes lived in round shaped houses called "wigwams." The people of the tribe believed and feared the Hobbamock. This being is said to come out at night and lurk in the shadows. Described as "hideous" and the Indian Boogeyman to some. It is said that those who have great faith in spirit, did not have to fear or be intimidated by this being. The Mohegan Tribe is a federally recognized tribe and sovereign tribal nation. There is a museum that features woodland artifacts in Connecticut and is operated by the Mohegan Tribe. The best part of the museum would be its tour, guided by Mohegan Tribe members.

WHEN IN CONNECTICUT, be on the lookout for the Melon Heads. Legend has it, there is a group of inbred large headed cannibals, living in the outskirt areas of Connecticut. Eyewitnesses have described them as small child-like humanoids with large, oversized craniums. They stay in hiding for the most part but have been known to attack if they feel threatened or seen by human eyes. It is believed they survive by consuming small rodents, roadkill and even their own. There are plenty of theories on how they came to be, but the most popular and talked about theory would be the evil doctor and his experiments that went horribly wrong. It is said that an extremely disturbed doctor named "Crow," had a goal to experiment on children for his sick amusement. Crow who was from Ohio, took in orphans that he believed no one would miss, and then performed heinous experiments upon them.

The procedures ended up making their brain swell, which is believed to be the reason for the deformity. These procedures also stopped the growth of the child. It is said the Melon Heads ended up in Connecticut, because they were transported out of Ohio, and left in the outskirts of the state in an attempt to not be linked back to Crow and his disgusting lab. Other states are now speaking up about witnesses that are coming forward. Stating they too have in fact seen or been attacked by a Melon Head, in the outskirts area of the state they reside.

—

BE AWARE, of a large creature lurking and following people in the Tunxis State Forest area of Hartford County. At this point a name has not been assigned so I will refer to the creature as "The River Mystery."

Near the state line dividing Connecticut from Massachusetts is a thick wooded area that the Hubbard River runs through. In the evening hours one hot Saturday night, two brothers were fishing along the river just off Route 20. It was a spot they have frequented for years so they were very familiar with their surroundings and the wildlife in the area. As they relaxed and cast their lines, out of nowhere came a loud splashing sound down the river. It was dark so they shone their flashlight in the direction of the sound. What they saw shocked and startled them. It was huge figure that crossed the river and was going up the hill side at a fast rate of speed.

It never stopped, it seemed to have no trouble getting to the top and then just disappeared out of view. The only sound it made was the sound of breaking branches as it climbed the side of the hill. According to the two brothers, they left and came back the next day to look around the area. There was no evidence of the creature they witnessed. They scoured the area looking for footprints, and hair but came up empty. There was nothing they could find to validate their sighting. They know what they saw, and who were at one point two skeptics, they now believe. They still fish at the spot when possible, but this time they are equipped with a camera in case they get so lucky to encounter another one of Americas mysteries.

9

Sussex County, DE
ROUTE 1 BEAST

DELAWARE ESTABLISHED its statehood in 1787 and was the 1st state to join the union. Its capital is Dover. It just happens to be the second smallest state at 2,489 square miles in the country, but very dense with a population of approximately nine-hundred-thousand. The state unlike most, only has three counties. From north to south, New Castle, Kent and Sussex which were all established in 1682.

Delaware is also home to the Delaware Indians. The Delaware Indians were known as the "Lenni Lenape Indians." The Delaware had a network of villages that each had their own hunting territories. Their territories were mostly located near streams and rivers such as the Delaware River. The Delaware men's attire would consist of deerskin cloth or fur which was referred to as breechcloths. The Delaware women traditionally would wear knee length dresses that wrapped around their body. The tribes people spoke of a large creature that would roam the land. It is said to be of a spirit form but could become earthly and abduct women and children if they wandered away from the village without first consulting with the leaders for a prayer of protection.

When visiting Delaware, be sure to visit the Zwaanendael Museum, to witness the famous mermaid they have on display. The foot-long mummified creature has been on display at the location since the early 1940s. Mermaid myth and lore, was first revealed in ancient mythological times. Described as half human from head to torso, then dolphin-like to the bottom of the tail. Its majestic beauty is intriguing to the eye, and its authority over all creatures of the sea speaks of mighty power. The subject fascinates and is studied by many in the Cryptozoology field. It is believed that they have rescued sailors from drowning when their ships capsized. Saved children who ventured out too far, and were being overcome by the fierce waves of the sea. Others claim, they have intervened and prevented shark attacks on humans.

HOWEVER, there seems to be an evil and devious version of this such creature referred to as "Sirens." In fact, there are more recorded attacks on humans over the years, and disappearances which have been attributed to the Sirens. It is said that the mermaids/sirens would seduce unsuspecting males with a seductive song, luring the man into the water. The male falls for the ploy, and enters the sea making his way toward what he believes is a woman standing alone, looking for companionship. The lower half of her body covered and hidden by the sea; he falls victim to her scheme. Once close enough, she lunges forward, embedding her long sharp claws into the victim. As the individual screams in fear and agony, they are pulled under the water where death is imminent.

No one can say for sure what happens to the bodies after the attack. In some cultures, it is believed they feed the creatures of the sea with the corpse, while others believe they themselves feast upon the body. In such a large unexplored sea, we may never know the full truth.

—

BE WARNED, if in Delaware you may see more than just a mermaid on display and cornfields. Some have witnessed the "Route 1 Bigfoot." Seen in the Sussex County territory near the Brumbley Family Park Campground and is said to be seven to eight-feet-tall with brown fur.

In the summer of 2010, a family was on vacation staying at the campground. They were at the end of their stay and packed up and set to head out. As they exited the campground onto Route 1 heading north, they came up to a corn field on the right side of the car. The stalks of corn stood high and looked to be a thick and healthy crop. The woman in the passenger seat watched the corn as they drove by. She noticed a figure walking in the stalks who ducked down as they passed. This would not normally seem strange, but the fact the stalks looked to stand over six-feet-tall and it only came up to the chest on the figure. The woman immediately asked her husband if he had witnessed what she saw, but he had not. To this day she cannot confirm or deny if this was in fact the Route 1 Bigfoot.

10

Miami Dade County, FL
GREEN SWAMP APE

FLORIDA NICKNAMED THE "SUNSHINE STATE," found its statehood in 1845. It was the 27th state to join the union. Its capital is Tallahassee and has a population of approximately nineteen million with a land mass of 65,758 square miles. Residents of the northern colder states tend to invade the state to get away from the colder temperatures. Others flock the state to visit Disney World located in Orlando. Disney opened in 1971 and is to date the largest and most visited resort and recreation park. The park stretches over 30,500 acres and attracts up to fifty-million visitors a year. Sea World another popular attraction in the Sunshine State opened in 1973, just two years after Disney World opened.

The Miccosukee Tribe has been an important part of Florida's history. The language of the Miccosukee is Mikasuki. The tribesmen were known for hunting deer, rabbits, wild turkeys and even alligators. The women would take on most of the farming tasks which included beans and corn. Shelters for the tribe has changed over the years. At one point in history, they lived in a style like hammock called "Chikees" which was made up of wood, plaster, and different types of fibers. The men wore breech cloths and tribal tattoos. The women traditionally wore skirts made from various types of fibers collected. The men in most cases had a shaved head what was called a "scalplock." The women had long hair and usually had it up in a bun type style. The people of the tribe told of a great dragon type being, that was said to inhabit the local swamp areas. The tribe's men would leave food such as fish they caught at the water's edge as a form of gifts to the creature. This was said to keep the beast from becoming hungry and eating the tribe's people.

———

WHEN ONE THINKS of Sasquatch in Florida, it is usually the infamous "Skunk Ape." The name comes from having an odor very similar to a skunk. Some say it smells this way due to seeking refuge in alligator holes. Some believe certain gases permeating from the ground in the swamps, is the cause of the odor. The Skunk Ape legend originated from Native American lore. The tribes people witnessed, and had many encounters with the creature, passing along stories over the decades. They respect the creature by not disturbing it.

The beast in fact is intelligent in its way of thinking, when choosing where to reside. Thick swampland is a perfect location to remain hidden, and ideal for such a creature of its size. This allows it to move freely and escape from human interaction quite easily. Also, it gives the beast an advantage when hunting and chasing down an animal type food source. The swampy area also provides a vegetation source of nutrition to survive.

———

ONE NOT SO FAMOUS, yet still seen is what I refer to as the "Green Swamp Ape." Said to stand seven-and-a-half-feet-tall, having green mossy colored fur and permeates a vial skunk smell. Could it be the "Skunk Ape," a family member or just merely another creature lurking the area? Nevertheless, skunk ape or not it has been seen multiple times by many in the Everglade region of Miami Dade County.

In 2015 a young couple were out on a date and took a ride down the Pa-Hay Okee Road. Approximately around 10:15 pm they arrived at the Pa-Hay Okee Look Out Tower. The tower sits deep in the Everglades and is a popular spot for young people. They parked the car and according to them started doing what young couples do when alone in a car. A few minutes later there was a loud bang on the passenger side of the car. The young man jumped out of the car and ran to the side. He saw a huge dent in the door and a large stone laying near the front tire. He looked around but could not see anyone or anything.

As he was walking around the front of the car, he noticed a horrible smell and heard a rustling in the bushes. Concerned about getting hit with a stone as he assumed it was a someone messing with them, he hurried, jumped in the car, and put up the window. He started the car in a hurry to get out of the area. When he turned on the head lights, about twenty-feet from the car in a thick area of bushes stood what he described as something resembling the incredible Hulk. It stood around eight-feet-tall, was dark green and looked mossy covered. Its shoulder width was around four-feet-wide. The creature let out a loud vocal that was low and guttural yet ended with a high pitch. The young man's date screamed, he put the car in drive and sped off. The sighting was not brought to the authorities' attention as the young couple had been smoking an illegal substance and feared having charges brought up on them.

Also, it was said that the area where the encounter occurred, they should not have been there in the time frame that they were.

11

Macon County, GA
PEEPING BIGFOOT

GEORGIA, whose capital is Atlanta was granted its statehood in 1788 and was the 4th state to join the union. Its population is approximately just under ten million with an area covering 59,425 square miles. Georgia was named after George II who was the king of Britain in 1733. At one time Georgia had the largest number of plantations of any state in the South. Georgia can be found north of Florida and touches the Atlantic Ocean.

The Creek Indians, unlike most tribes did not move a lot. They were not a nomadic tribe but would rather set up hut-like shelters. They would usually set these homes in villages. They would hold many events that would consist of dancing and community meetings. However, if a village grew too large, they would split into two separate villages. History speaks that they kept close to one another even after moving. The Creek diet would consist of fish, wild turkey, deer, and bison. Corn was also another important part of their diet. They were known to have common weapons for fighting and hunting such as bow and arrow, spears, tomahawks, and clubs. The men and women wore similar clothing that was sophisticated in nature.

It is said that the Creek Indians wore jewelry and antlers as part of their wardrobe. The people feared Isti Papa, which was described by the people as a giant bear-cat creature that is said to be cannibalistic in nature. It was witnessed mostly in the form of a spirit but could also turn physical. Many Creek folks who vanished, were believed to have fallen victim to this creature.

IF EVER IN the state of Georgia to hunt, be on the lookout for the beast known as Hogzilla. The creature first made its appearance in 2004. Its a wild boar said to be over twelve-feet-long, weighing well over one-thousand-pounds. Many hunters, hikers and campers have claimed to be chased off by what they described as an unusually large hog. Many accounts have claimed the hog ravaged through occupied camp sites, and fears no human. One hiker claimed, the hog came out of a thick area of bushes and began to charge him. The hikers only escape was to climb up a nearby tree, and wait for the animal to leave. It has been claimed that a hunter shot and killed the hog. Even if this is true, and the beast has been exterminated, who's to say there is only one?

ALSO BE on the lookout for a creature even Hogzilla would fear. Known to one person as the "Peeping Bigfoot," because of its behavior of looking into windows, it is brown in color, and stands eight-feet-tall.

A woman in Macon County near Willow Lake, was home with her son and newborn baby. The father was at work as he was scheduled for a 2nd shift at his place of employment. As the woman sat on her couch in their living room, she saw a shadowy figure walk by one of the windows. Living in the country, they often had wild animals pass through their property, so she was not initially concerned. Shortly after, she heard a noise like a large bird hitting the side of the house. It was loud enough that it woke up the baby. From the other side of the house, she could hear the baby crying. She walked into the baby's room and stopped dead in her tracks. Looking in a window that was no less than seven-feet from the ground was a large figure. It had red glowing eyes and it seemed to fog up the window as it breathed.

It then left the window. The woman grabbed the baby, and claimed she called her husband and the police. The police and her husband arrived about the same time. They searched the property but found nothing. The authorities felt it was a peeping tom and possibly looked big in the window from the light of the moon casting a shadow. The woman has yet to have another experience like this, but now has a loaded shot gun in place for if whatever she saw, returns.

12

Honolulu County, HI
WAHIAWA GIANT

HAWAII, whose capital is Honolulu became the 50th US State in 1959. Some call or have nick-named this sought-after travel destination the "Big Island." Hawaii is made up of a group of volcanic islands in the central Pacific Ocean. It has a population of approximately one and a half million with an area covering 10,926 square miles. There was a population increase in the 1900s with the expansion of plantations with systems to grow sugar cane and pineapples. On December 7, 1941, Japanese fighter planes attacked the American naval base at Pearl Harbor killing over 2000 American soldiers. This propelled the US into World War II.

The Hawaiians are of their own tribe in many way's. The people believe that they were created by "The Mother Earth and "Father the Sky." It translates to or defines the names as "Wakea" and "Papa." The Hawaiians take land and family very seriously. The word "Ohana" is used for family and the word "Aina" is used for land. It has been said that "family" to Hawaiians is not defined by just bloodline or immediate family, but by the well-being and prosperity of the whole group. A Hawaiian is not just someone who lives in the area, but

43

someone who shares in the traditions and cultures. The Hawaiians believe in many different types of gods. "Lono" is the Hawaiian god for rain. Rain helps to keep their land fertile and helps in their agriculture. It is said that the Kalo plant is a symbol of their Hawaiian native god. The Kanaka Maoli Tribe are the native Hawaiians of the "truest sense."

IF EVER LUCKY enough to have a getaway to this beautiful destination, the locals will tell you to be on the lookout for "the Menehunes." The legend describes them as, two to three-foot-tall dwarf-like people. Said to exist for years, they are also known to be hard workers and constantly building. They are nocturnal in nature, so all activities and work are completed by only the light of the moon. It's warned, not to touch anything they built, as they are very territorial and will attack. In the year 1820, the Island of Kauai had sixty-five individuals listed on the islands census as actual, Menehune little people.

ANOTHER LEGEND LIVES in the Wahiawa Mountains and known to some as "the Wahiawa Giant" or "Aikanaka." Described as an eight-foot-tall hairy Wildman, witnessed many times running down trails of the mountain. Some say it has been seen wearing a loin cloth at times. Many also say that prior to seeing the beast in most cases they will hear the scream, which no one can really describe as it is so terrifying. Legend has it that a giant man would terrorize the people. Some say it is a spirit that roams the land. There were no exact accounts to reference in this case, so we brought to light this legend.

13

Adams County, ID
CAMPER SHAKER

IDAHO, whose capital is the famous Boise achieved its statehood in 1890 and was the 43rd state to join the union. When one thinks of Idaho, usually the potato comes to mind. A popular potato grown in the state is the Russet Burbank. The weather in the state makes it an ideal environment for growing large crops. Idaho yields the largest yearly crop of potatoes in the country second in the hot potato game only to Washington State which does in fact produce more. Idaho is twice as large as the six New England states combined. Its capital Boise is a large city with over 200,000 residents. The state yields a population of approximately 1.7 million. Idaho boarders Canada and is 83,568 square miles.

The Blackfoot tribe, also known as "Blackfeet," is said by some to be a fierce, warlike tribe that calls themselves the "Real People." The name Blackfoot came about due to the routine they have of blackening their moccasins with ash. The tribe flies a blue flag to mark their reservation. The men of the tribe were the hunters and buffalo are considered one of the most valued animals. They would use them for many things such as food shelter and clothing. Other animals hunted are deer, elk, and moose. The women of the tribe would overlook the needs of the household with preparing food and most of the cleaning. The tribes lived in house like huts usually made up of buffalo hides and were called "tipis." History states that it was easy to set up. Today, they live-in modern-day houses. The Blackfoot tribe members spoke of a fearsome water-monster named "Omahksoyisksiksina." The creature described as a large horned snake, lurks in the depths of the lakes and rivers. It is claimed to have an appetite for human flesh. Most deaths having to do with drowning, have been blamed on the horned snake creature.

———

IF EVER IN Idaho and plan to spend the day on the Payette Lake, be on the lookout. Witnessed in the lake by many locals is a creature that resembles one of the Loch Ness Monster. The serpent was given the name of "Sharlie," in the 1950s. There were in fact sightings in earlier years, but a name was not rightfully given immediately. The first documented sighting was in the 1920s. The bizarre creature is described as almost fifty-feet-long, slimy in appearance with brownish green scales from head to tail. Some claim it is just a floating log that gets pulled down from an undercurrent in the water which makes it look like its diving and swimming. Others claim they first saw what appeared to be a snake-like head peer out of the water. Followed by three to four half circle humps. This occurrence would happen multiple times in a row before it would then disappear into the depths of the water. According to the folks who live on the shore, they all have a heart for the creature and consider it to be "gentle," considering there has never to this day, been a recorded incident of any attack or violent behavior.

———

THE SAME CANNOT be said for what locals in the Adams County region would tell you about a creature that lurks and calls the area home. Described as bipedal standing seven and a half to eight-feet-tall and weighing in at around six-hundred-pounds. Dark brown fur covers the beast, and it like many others permeates an odor described as rotting roadkill mixed with skunk. It is said that it also has a bellowing vocal that is deep and guttural.

A man was looking forward to hunting season and was camping out in the woods. There was a certain area he would stay each year and always had luck taking down wild game. Calling it his "lucky spot," he was excited to get back in the area and set up. He arrived at the location in the evening time around 6 pm so he still had day light in his favor. Being in the woods, away from it all, could be called his happy place, until this very day. He set up camp, his tent, and his belongings. He went out and started to gather wood for a fire. As he walked around about 100 yards for his camp, he noticed a horrible skunk like odor that made his eyes water, and his nostrils burn.

He looked around to see if there was any signs or movement from a skunk. He came up empty, so he took the kindling he had found and carried it back to his site. He set up a place for his fire and produced a flame. As the fire grew, he cleaned and loaded his shot gun. He then cooked some food over the fire. He consumed the burnt food, then sat by the glowing flame, and relaxed. As the sun set the dark began to roll in, the man started to get ready to sleep, and set his alarm to awaken early to start his routine. He climbed into his shelter tent, laid down and fell asleep. Shortly, he was awakened by a loud guttural groan in the distance. Assuming it to be a bear he grabbed his gun. He waited; it was silent. He laid back down and was about to close his eyes when he heard the groan again, but this time it sounded possibly to be only around 20 yards away. He unzipped his tent and stepped out with a flashlight. He shone the light around the area but saw nothing.

He waited a few minutes, but with no more activity, he re-entered the tent. As he sat there, he suddenly could hear something walking outside of the tent. Whatever it was it made the deep groan vocal. At the same time, he noticed the same awful smell he experienced earlier in the day. He yelled out and heard the unidentified creature run off. He sat there for a few minutes, when he felt it was safe to exit, he stepped out to investigate. He shone the flashlight around and could see nothing. He sat out for a while in anticipation of whatever it was returning. It never came back. He entered back into the tent and with his gun by his side he fell asleep. The next morning, he exited the tent and as he walked around the site, he noticed what appeared to be a large footprint. It was described as in the twenty-two-inch realm.

Thinking what had passed through his camp that night was not a bear, he decided to tear down his tent, pack up and leave the area. He has been back to what at one point was called his lucky spot, but never alone, always with another hunter. To this day there has not been another incident like he experienced that one evening.

14

Madison County, IL
DOUGLAS

ILLINOIS, whose capital is Springfield, found its statehood in 1818. It was the 21st state to join the union. There was the fire in 1871 in Chicago that many believed would stunt the growth of the city, but the metropolis continued to grow with thousands of individuals migrating to the state to work in the mills, slaughterhouses, and rail yards. Its approximate population is around thirteen million. A full 80% of the area is considered farmland, but the state in a whole is 57,916 square miles. The state is also home to the Nabisco plant that is considered the largest bakery in the world at 1,800,000 square feet. If you have ever heard of the "Lincoln Coin" it originated in Illinois. It is a picture of Lincoln on the front hold a book. Could this state also be the birthplace of the ice cream sundae? Some say, "Absolutely."

When visiting the state, you will often hear of the Algonquian Indians. The Algonquian lived in a couple different types of shelters. It mostly would depend on the season of the year. In the colder months they would dwell in a type of house that was made from wood and bark. In the warmer months they would stay in what is described as dome like tents made up of animal hides and held up with makeshift poles. The people of the tribe would use bow and arrow, knives, and spears while hunting. They would hunt for such animals as, beaver, bear, moose, deer, and elk. They would also fish, using spears to stab the fish as they swam by. The Algonquin would use fur from animals they trapped to clothe themselves. In the summer months they would wear hides of deerskin with loin cloths. When the seasons would change to the colder months, they would simply just add to what they were already wearing for extra warmth. Like most tribes, the men did the hunting, while the women took care of the gardening, cooking, cleaning, and childcare.

The people of the tribes feared what they described as a mythical flying creature. Described as a flying snake-like serpent with a wide wingspan. The creature has been said to ambush its prey from above and carry it away. Young children were said to be the most to fall victim of this monster. The tribe's people would protect all children and would warn all to stay together and always watch the skies.

ILLINOIS, with its booming population and rich history is also home to what folks call the "Enfield Horror." The creature has been described as some type of deformed extraterrestrial looking humanoid beast. The bizarre appearance sets it apart from many other legendary creatures. The most common description given from eyewitness accounts, state standing five to six-feet-tall walking on three oddly shaped legs, hunched over and having two-to-three-foot-long thin arms. The feet and hands looking similar in appearance and resembling a lizard type claw with narrow long thin nails. The skin is described as rough scale-like and gray in color. Some describe the creature as having some type of "out of this world" alien facial appearance. This includes having red glowing eyes. The first recorded encounter of this such abomination in Enfield took place in 1973 by a young boy. From then on, the creature would wreak havoc upon on the people of the small-town attacking animals, adults and even more children. The encounters consisted of the creature chasing and trying to grab whoever came in reaching distance. Some claim the creature would bang on the side of houses while letting out an indescribable scream. Others claim the creature would use its sharp nails, and claw at windows and doors. Since the original out-break of terror, the sightings have been far and few, yet the folks of the small rural town have not forgotten, and still speak of the creature often.

The legend of the Enfield Horror is in fact frightening, but locals of Madison County believe another just as frightening being exists in the wooded forests surrounding the area. The creature is named "Douglas" for the simple fact there has been many eyewitnesses who while driving down New Douglas Road have encountered a road crossing. The beast has been described as between seven-feet-tall. All black fur, with a narrow cone shaped head. Some say it could weigh in at a whopping eight hundred pounds. Some have described the creature to have red glowing eye's which is common with Sasquatch sightings across the globe.

In the early morning hours in 2017, a woman was out delivering newspapers. She was heading west towards the town of Livingston. Just before the Silver Creek area she noticed a large "something" standing near the side of the road. She slowed down concerned that it was a bear or moose and might jump out in front of her. As she approached, it darted out across the road running on two legs. It took only two strides to get from one side of the road to the other, and then disappeared out of sight. As the woman drove by where it seemed to vanish, she slowed and rolled down her window. She said she could hear something large crashing through the woods but could see nothing.

15

Morton County, IN
BLACK APE

INDIANA, whose capital is Indianapolis found its statehood in 1816. It was the 19th state of the union. Indiana is a small state at 36,417 square miles with a population of approximately 6.5 million residents. In 1866 the first ever train robbery in the United States took place in Indiana. Some fun attractions to visit if ever in the state would be visiting the Indianapolis Zoo, the Indianapolis Speedway and the Children's museum. In 1883 two young boys happen to come across some caves which are now open to the public to visit called The Marengo Caves. Indiana is also home to "Dead Con" which is held in October every year.

The Shawnee Indians are known as Northeast American Indian Tribes. The Shawnee men were responsible for protecting their families and going to war if needed. The men also did the fishing and hunting for the family. The people would eat whatever they could catch but preferred buffalo, deer, and wild turkey. They would use spears, bow, and arrow and nets. The women took care of the home and the children. This included all cooking, cleaning, and farming of a variety of foods. The women would also fill their time with weaving rugs and using hemp to create ropes. The tribe is known for creating outer wear that was more basic, not as elaborate but certainly did the job it was required to do. The women mostly wore wrap around skirts with a type of legging while the men wore the more traditional breechcloths.

The Shawnee people believed in the "Kokumthena." Described as a supernatural being that is said to be female. The being is considered a grandmother to the tribe but is also considered to be a goddess type spirit.

⎯⎯

IF VISITING Indiana and love to swim, avoid the Ohio River in Evansville. In 1955 a couple of young women made the first claim of a creature lurking in the water. Stating one was attacked while swimming. The creature is now known as the "Green Clawed Beast." Described as resembling the aquatic monster the "Creature from the Black Lagoon," from the 1954 Hollywood classic. Some have described the creature as resembling the creature from "The Swamp Thing," from the 1982 film. Another encounter occurred while in the late 1960s when four women were enjoying the sounds of nature while taking a leisurely swim in the river. Two of the women were on shore while the others enjoyed the cooling and relaxing flow of the water. When out of nowhere, one young woman felt a large, webbed hand grab her ankle. It attempted to pull her under the water. She could feel sharp claw-like nails dig firmly into her skin. She screamed and kicked as the beast made every attempt to subdue her. At one point she believed she would not survive, but right at that moment she was able to break free from the grasp and swim to shore.

Her leg was bruised and had deep gashes in the area the monster held her. While she was swimming to shore, two of her friends that were on land saw a dark green humanoid figure rise out of the water and then slowly sink back down beneath the surface. They packed up their belongings and ran as fast as they could back to their cars never to return. Since this incident, thrill seekers still swim in the river, regardless of the history, disregarding the dangers. To this day, there have been more claims of creature attacks in the rivers water.

———

ALSO, they fear what some call the "Black Ape." Said to be seven to eight-feet-tall with fur being jet black. It also gets its name from the fact it walks hunched over how one would see an ape walk. In the summer of 2008, a gentleman was out sitting on his back deck that overlooked a thick and dense wooded area. It was sometime between 9 and 10 pm. As he sat taking in the peaceful surroundings, he heard some rustling in a bushy section of the tree line about thirty yards away. He watched for a minute or so. It stopped and went silent again. Living in this area it was not uncommon for wild animals to roam his property. A few minutes later his wife let their dog out who sat by his side for a few minutes, then went off the deck into the yard. Shortly after, the dog began to growl at the same area the man heard the rustling earlier. The dog began to bark in the direction.

The man concerned that it was a skunk or animal that might attack his dog, got up and grabbed the dog by its collar. As he was walking back towards the house, he heard a snarl like sound. He turned around but could not believe what he was seeing. It was a large hunched over figure with yellow eyes. It had broad shoulders and appeared to have no neck. The dog took off and ran up on the porch whimpering. The man followed right behind his dog. He ran into the house and grabbed his shot gun. When he arrived back outside, the creature was gone. The man wanting to make sure it left, shot in the direction where he saw it standing. There was no noise just the remaining echo of the shot he took. Since that day he has not seen the creature again but will hear strange unidentifiable howls from time to time.

16

Jefferson County, IA
SKUNK RIVER SASQUATCH

IOWA, whose capital is Des Moines gained its statehood in 1846 as the 29th state to join the union. Iowa is 56,273 square miles with a population of approximately three million residents. Folks come from other states to visit such attractions as the Iowa State fair, the National Mississippi River Museum and Aquarium as well as the Boone and Scenic Valley Railroad.

Iowa is also home of the "Fox Tribe." The Fox tribe were warlike people who were extremely fierce. They were originally found inhabiting the territory in the western Great Lakes Region. The Fox people were hunters, farmers, and fisherman. The people would hunt to feast on fish, deer, elk, bear, and even smaller animals such as squirrels, turtles, and raccoons. They would also farm such foods as corn and squash. The people wore breech cloths, buckskin leggings, moccasins and a robe or blanket type of robe. They lived in temporary shelters called a longhouse. The longhouses had wooden roofs with doors on both sides of the shelter. There was also a "smoke hole" in the middle to allow light and air in. The wigwam shelter was cone shaped with a wooded frame and could easily be set up and taken down. The Fox people spoke of a serpent-like creature with a horned head. It is an underwater serpent that latches his prey and pulls to the depths. It has been said to be up to fifty-feet-long with a body width comparable to a telephone pole. Many unexplained events and disappearances were blamed on this such creature. It is said that the creature is a curse from the sky God for immoral behavior that mankind was guilty of partaking in.

If like the Fox tribe and you are into eating small prey like turtles, make sure you bring a large net to catch this monster size hard shelled legend. Known as the "Monster Turtle of Blue Pond," this enormous creature has been witnessed by countless individuals. Some accounts claim the turtle to be as large as a small compact car. There have been claims made that the turtle has attacked swimmers and tried to pull them under water. There is no real documented information to confirm this such claim. The Pond can be found in Clear Lake State Park and is over thirty-feet-deep. So, if interested in seeing this monster turtle, stop in.

———

ANOTHER CREATURE TO be on the lookout for is what the folks of Jefferson County call the "Skunk River Sasquatch." Getting its name from being seen in the Skunk River Valley area, it is said to be over eight-feet-tall with reddish fur and leaving a musty rotten egg like odor wherever it roams. In the summer of 2007, a call "allegedly" came into the Jefferson County Sheriff's department regarding what was perceived to be a Bigfoot sighting. The caller described as he walked the Skunk River; he noticed a putrid odor. A few moments later there was a large splash noise down the river. Looking ahead he could not see anything so continued.

Suddenly there was another loud splash and this time the individual saw a large rock hit the water coming off from a rocky-like cliff area. As he looked at the top of the cliff, there was what he described as a large dark reddish figure about fifty-yards from him. He could not make out the face but being an avid outdoors man, he knew it was not a bear and it fit the description of a Bigfoot. They locked eyes, the figure retreated and disappeared out of sight.

17

Mitchell County, KS
GORILLA MAN

KANSAS, which is in what is called "The American Great Plains," established its statehood in 1861. Its capital is Topeka and has an approximate population of three million with an area covering 82,278 square miles. It was the 34th state to join the union. When one thinks of Kansas, most of us are reminded of the movie *The Wizard of Oz*. We think of Dorothy, To-To, the Yellow Brick Road, the Wicked Witch, Glinda and of course the Lolli Pop Kids. What we do not think of is the bloody path Kansas took to achieve statehood. Shortly after what was called the Kansas-Nebraska ACT of 1854 two territories opened to settlement and this allowed the new settlers to a choice whether the states could be admitted to the union as "slave" or as "free." This led to a lot of violence and the territory was known as "Bleeding Kansas." The state is home to the major US military installation Fort Leavenworth. If one is a White Castle or Pizza Hut lover, you will be happy to know that both were founded in Wichita.

Kansas is known for the Kansa Tribe. The Kansa men were hunters and would sometimes go to war in the event they needed to protect their families and loved ones. The Kansa women were farmers and did most of the cleaning and took care of the Kansa children. They lived in shelters known as "lodges" which were constructed with wooden type frames and were covered usually using branches with packed earth like material. The homes were usually larger than what most other tribes would construct due to the fact they preferred to have all family members live in the same home. Some homes could be as large as fifty-feet-across. The Kansa women wore wrap-around skirts with deerskin type shawls. The men wore leather leggings, breechcloths, and buckskin shirts. The tribe would hunt deer, buffalo as well as small game. The bow and arrow were their choice when hunting or going to war. The Kansa people spoke of the "Wakanda" which was a spirit who kept watch over the tribe's people. The spirit was said to punish those who broke tribal culture but would reward and protect the ones who held all traditions dear. Today, the Kansa people call the spirit the "Great Creator,' and associate and identify the spirit as the "Biblical God" spoken of in the bible.

In the times we now live in, we do not use bow and arrows when we go to war. Although it would be a good idea to have some kind of way to protect yourself if you ever visit Kansas, and come face to face with the infamous "Sink Hole Sam." Sinkhole Sam is a longtime legend from the area in Mcpherson County. It is said that Inman Lakes area was drained, leaving "sinkholes" behind. To the average eye, it appears to be just puddles on the ground. But in fact, they are deep wide holes that can drown a full-grown man. Within the sink holes lies what the people of the area report as a large fifteen-to-twenty-foot snake. Not only extremely long, but as wide as a telephone pole.

The creature is said to have been living within the lake in a cave type underwater tunnel system that connected to other lakes in across the country. This may explain why the large snake had never been seen prior. The underwater tunnels would be an extremely ideal hiding place and reason no one else had seen Sam prior to the lakes demise. Sam like most snakes has not ever attacked, but always tried to flee when a human encounter occurred.

———

ANOTHER CREATURE that one should be aware of would be the "Gorilla man" of Mitchell County. Reported to be in the nine-foot range, a few young women noticed a huge man-like creature in a corn field when they were driving down the road. They slowed down and as they did it seemed to drop down on all fours and disappeared behind the tall stalks of corn. According to the women they are convinced they saw a Bigfoot in the nine-foot range with black fur, but most believe it was a misidentification and it was a black bear.

18

Harlan County, KY
HARLAN COUNTY BIGFOOT

KENTUCKY, whose capital is Frankfort established its state-hood in 1792 and was the 15th state to join the union. Kentucky is also known by many as the "Blue Grass State." Its approximate population is 4.5 million and covers 40,411 square miles. Daniel Boone a popular Frontiersman was one of Kentucky's most prominent explorers. Kentucky is also known as a major US coal producer. When in the state you can drive by the US military bases Fort Campbell, and Fort Knox. You should also know that it is the home of the legendary Kentucky derby horse races and blue grass music, which was pioneered by Bill Monroe, a Kentucky native.

Kentucky is also home to the Yuchi Tribe. The Yuchi tribe would shelter themselves in small type houses set up in a village of similar type shelters. The homes are made up of a wooden structure packed with clay. They were known to build walls around the village to protect them from potential attacks. The Yuchi men were the hunters and used bow and arrow as well as blowguns. When fishing they used basket traps and spears. Yuchi women did the cleaning and most of the childcare. The tribesmen wore breechcloths with leggings, while the women wore the traditional wraparound skirts, usually made from deerskin or other fibers woven together. The Yuchi people were known for both men and women to help with farming such crops as squash and corn. It is said that storytelling and fairy tales are an important pass time for the Yuchi tribe. The Yuchi people are very brave, but they did however fear the "Tie-Snakes." It is said they live in the water and are the size of an average snake. However, the serpent is said to have unusual strength for its size and would target and catch humans to drown and devour. Today, the snakes are said to be just lore, which was passed down from generation to generation.

WHEN IN KENTUCKY, consider yourself warned. Watch where you venture off to, you could very well come across what the folks of the state call "The Devil Monkeys." Encounters with these creature's date back to the early 1930s. Some believe they are an unclassified species that science is aware of, but will not admit. They are described to stand bipedal at around four to five-feet-tall, with orange eyes. The face is said to resemble and have canine features. The growl also is very close to sounding like a large rabid dog. They are said to be extremely vicious, and fear nothing. Some claim that the creatures are paranormal, having the ability to slip out of sight, or disappear altogether.

Some encounters/attacks have taken place during daytime and at night. One attack took place in the late 1980s while a man was hiking. He was attacked from behind, but was able to turn around and see what he described as a large monkey-like animal with long nails. The creature was able to connect with the hiker leaving long deep gashes on his thigh. The attack ended and the being ran off. To this date no Devil Monkeys have been captured nor have there been any recent sighting.

If ever driving down the long stretch of rural highway 1137, also be on the lookout as you might just encounter the Harlan County Bigfoot. Witnessed by multiple travelers, there is one encounter that holds a lot of validity. In the mid 2000s at around 8pm, a young woman was traveling northeast on Route 1137 near the Crummies Creek area when she felt ill. Her head started to pound; and felt a lot of anxiety. As she looked to the right side of the road, she witnessed a large bi-pedal figure covered with black hair. It was very "ape-like" and as she approached, it retreated into the woods. The young woman did not stop, as she passed the area where the figure was standing and drove further down the road, her head no longer hurt and the anxiety she felt dissipated. To this day, she still drives down this stretch of road weekly, but has not seen the beast again nor has she ever felt the symptom's she experienced that evening. Was this a situation where infrasound was in play produced by an animal that effected this young woman? Or did she just have a headache? According to her, what she saw was indeed, a Bigfoot.

19

Rapides Parish, LA
THE AZALEA MONSTER

LOUISIANA, whose capital is Baton Rough achieved its statehood in 1812 as the 18th state to join the union. It is called by many the Pelican State. It carries a population of approximately 4.5 million residents with an area covering 51,988 square miles. Hurricane Katrina was a devastating storm that hit landfall in southeastern Louisiana on August 29, 2005. To date, this was the most destructive natural disaster in US history. It resulted in more than 1,800 deaths. Over 1,500 of which were in Louisiana and close to $100 billion in damages. The recovery time was long, but the people pulled together and united which in turn brought the state back. The Dixieland Jazz was soon back!

Other individuals you will hear about when speaking of Louisiana would be the Caddo tribe. The Caddo men were the hunters who primarily used bow and arrow and the women did the cooking, childcare, and farming. The Caddo people lived in round shaped grass houses or lodge type homes which had thatched roofs that were made from vegetation such as straw. The men wore the traditional breechcloth with leather type leggings, and moccasins. The women wore wrap around type skirts, often made from woven fibers or deerskin. The women also wore moccasins. Both genders wore earrings. If the Caddo men had to defend their families, they would have weapons such as tomahawks and spears. The Caddo people were also famous for their artistry in their creation of decorated pots. The tribes people told tales of little people that were believed to be spirits or ghosts. The fear spread through the villages and it was said to not go into the woods alone, as they might take you. Also, do not get lost while in the forest, they will use one's fear against them and according to Caddo folklore, the individual will never be seen again.

THERE IS no doubt in my mind that if one is into Sasquatch, or any type of creature or monster, they are familiar with the Louisiana lore and have heard of the "Honey Island Swamp Monster." This Bigfoot type creature has been talked about for decades. Described as standing seven-feet-tall and covered with grey hair. The eyes of the creature are said to sit way back in the creature's head and have a glowing yellow hue to them. The creature is also said to have a decaying flesh-like odor permeating the surrounding air. No one really knows how it migrated into the state, but one theory is a train derailed that was carrying wild animals and an ape escaped. To this day this theory has not been proven and in most cases not taken seriously. The Louisiana swamps are known for unusual and mysterious lights hovering over the Bayou. Some claim they are the ghosts of Native Americans that once lived in the area, and they guide and protect the swamp monster.

THERE IS another creature that lurks standing about seven-and-a-half-feet-tall that is known as the "Azalea Monster." Off Route 488 in Rapids Parish area back in the late 90s, four young men met up at the "Wild Azalea Trail Head," in the early evening hours. It was a Friday night, and they were going over the plans for the evening. As they spoke one of the young men heard movement in the woods. Not thinking much about, it he said nothing. A few moments later a rock came out of the woods and hit one of the cars, denting the hood. The young men turned around and stared off in the direction the rock came from. The one who owned the car that the rock hit, yelled out some obscenities and explained this was his parent's car. They started down the trail that led into the woods. At about fifty-feet in, they heard a roar that seemed to shake the ground. Also, to their surprise, they heard sticks breaking and what sounded like a large animal making its way quickly through the woods. It was dark so no one was able to identify what was making the noise. Immediately they turned, ran to the cars, and drove off. The next day they went during the day to see if they could find any clues to what was in the woods. There was what could be described as a "partial footprint," but it could not be confirmed.

20

Oxford County, ME
BI-PEDAL CROSSER

MAINE, NICKNAMED "VACATIONLAND," is the largest of the six New England States. Maine became the 23rd state to join the US in 1820. Its capital is Augusta and covers 35,384 square miles, with an approximate population of 1.5 million residents. Most who vacation in New Hampshire will also make a trip into Maine to visit such beaches as Olde Orchard and Wells. Maine is popular for its rocky and beautiful coastlines. If you love blueberries, Maine is the leading producer. Also, one cannot visit Maine without feasting on a lobster. Maine is in fact, the largest US producer of lobster.

The Maliseet Tribe is a well know group of people if you ask anyone from Maine. They would build shelters known as wigwams, which is described as a small round building. The tribesmen wore breechcloths with leggings, while the women wore long dresses with sleeves that could be removed. Both male and female wore moccasins. The Maliseet people were considered river people, so they were master fisherman. They also hunted deer and moose. Usually, the men did all the hunting while the women took care of the children and most of the cleaning. The men when out hunting for food, would use bow and arrow for land game and what is described as pronged spears while fishing. Today some Maliseet people still wear moccasins and have adopted some fashion adding beads to the shoes and shirts. The people of the tribe had to always be on the lookout for a creature that many describe as a large "wolf-like" man. This deadly wolverine monster would ambush its prey. Stealth in its movement, anyone who fell victim to the beast never saw it approaching until it was too late. It is said that even if you did get a glimpse of the creature, you would be so frightened that you could not move. Many disappearances have been blamed on this creature.

WHILE VISITING MAINES BEAUTIFUL COASTLINE, and you ask about Cassie, you will be surprised how well known this creature is to the people of the state. Cassie has been seen all along the coast of Maine, many times from 1912 to the present day. Some refer to her as the Casco Bay Sea Serpent of Maine. Cassie has been described as a large serpent like creature estimated to be one-hundred-feet-long, with a plesiosaurus type neck. The center belly area of the creature is said to be the size of a large barrel and the whole body a dark green color. It has been reported that Cassie can swim at an extremely high speed, keeping up alongside boats. There have been no reported sightings in the last few decades of Cassie. The locals hope and believe that one day, the creature will in fact show again.

ANOTHER TERRIFYING CREATURE lurks in Maine, but not on the coastline, but by land. This bi-pedal creature standing nearly nine-feet-tall has been seen by many. A truck driver was out in the early morning hours traveling on Route 2 in Oxford County. He had just passed the Stony Brook Campground when he saw a large figure run out in front of his truck. It all happened so fast. By the time he hit the brakes he had felt a thud. Not totally sure what he had hit and concern it could be human the way it ran out, he quickly grabbed a flashlight and jumped out of the truck to investigate. As he arrived at the front of the vehicle, he could hear something crashing through the woods. The front grill of the truck had been broken. He shone the flashlight in the direction he could hear whatever it was he hit running but could see nothing. Soon the noise stopped so he called the incident into his dispatcher.

21

Kent County, MD
KENT TRACKER

MARYLAND, known to some as The Old-Line State or The Free State. Achieved its statehood in 1788 and was the 7th state to join the union. Maryland can be found in the center of the eastern seaboard. Its capital is Annapolis. The capital is also home to the United States Naval Academy. It has an approximate population of 5.8 million residents, while covering an area of 12,406 square miles. This state is known for its renowned crab cakes and said to be the leading producer of blue crabs.

In Maryland, there is the Susquehannock Tribe. The men hunted elk, bison, deer, and bear. The women would butcher the animals, smoke the meat, and prepared the hides. The men wore deerskin loincloths, leggings with moccasins. When it was colder outside, they would wear bearskin robes. The women kept their hair long, and wore deerskin dresses, leggings with moccasins. The Susquehannock tribe told stories of a wild and hairy cannibalistic creature that roamed the lands. Said to be eight-feet in height with a slender build. The tribes people still speak of this creature's lore today, but many believe it was a Sasquatch.

———

SNALLYGASTER. I have no idea where that name came from. Regardless of where the name originated, the description of the Snallygaster from witnesses are certainly bone chilling. It is described as a fearsome dragon-like flying beast. A large reptilian bird, it has a long neck and sharp dagger-like beak that some say has a silver to metallic like shine. Witnesses describe the wingspan as up to thirty-feet from tip to tip, and has sharp claw-like nails said to be up to six-inches in length. It's reported that large horns or tentacles are protruding from the top of its head and on each side of its body. There are reports that the beast has a third eye in the middle of its fore-head, that glows red. It's reported that prior to laying eyes on the creature, one will first hear loud screeching and another sound of explosion like thunderclaps. This source of warning has saved many lives. It's reported that the creature will swoop down from the stars and feast on pets, farm animals, and even children. It's believed to have been around thousands of years ago, but a preserved egg in the mountain area had hatched, releasing this such creature in the early 1900s. So, watch the skies.

———

WHILE YOU KEEP an eye on the sky, also keep an eye out for a nosey Bigfoot in Kent County. In 2013 around 2am in the morning, a woman was awakened by a strange feeling that she was not alone. Feeling extremely uncomfortable, she sat up in her bed. When she did, she saw a large silhouette of something looking in her window. It had red eyes and immediately retreated. As it left, she could hear grunting. The bottom sill of the window the creature was peering into, was at the eight-foot mark. This would lead us to believe that it was not a human, and whatever it was stood a minimum of nine-feet-tall. The woman called a friend, not the police in fear of ridicule. He walked around the house and according to the woman, found what appeared to be a large footprint near the window and another in the direction that she believes it fled. The woman still lives in the house, and to this day has not had any other encounters. She has since purchased a shot gun.

22

Hampden County, MA
NYE BROOK BIGFOOT

MASSACHUSETTS, part of the six New England states, achieved its statehood in 1788, and was the 6th state to join the union. Some call it the "Commonwealth State." Its capital is Boston which has had many historical events take place in the city such as the Boston Tea Party during the American Revolution, and the Boston Massacre. Its population is approximately 6.5 million. With that many residing in the state, it is hard to believe that Massachusetts is only 10,554 square miles. For all those Toll House Chocolate Chip Cookie lovers, in 1997 this cookie was designated as the official cookie of the Commonwealth.

Massachusetts is also home to the Wampanoag Tribe. The tribe's men, like most tribes were the hunters and used bow and arrows and heavy clubs. They hunted every type of animal but mostly deer and wild turkey. When fishing they used nets with hooks attached. The women did most of the cleaning, cooking and childcare. Both men and women would farm. The men would wear breechcloths with leggings, while the women would wear knee length skirts. Neither the men nor women had to wear shirts in their culture. The Wampanoag tribe were known for their arts and crafts. They would weave baskets, create wood carvings, and lay out bead work on clothing. The shelters they would build were called wetu or wigwams built in a central village like setting.

The people of the tribe feared what is referred to as the "Pukwudgie." It was believed that this creature could transform itself into different beings. It has been described as gray in color, small with glowing type skin. The creature is said to be in the troll family and resembles other types of lore little people.

━━━

ONE CRYPTID in Massachusetts lore is known as the Dover Demon. First making the news in the 1970s, it is said to be a humanoid like creature, with a large, disproportioned head, which held two large intense glowing orange eyes that have also been reported as green. The creature is extremely thin in stature and believed to be in the five-to-five-and-a-half-feet in height range. When moving, it has been witnessed by many, the creature hunching forward and walking on its long thin alien-like arms and legs. The fingers are said to be six-to-seven-inches-long with sharp thin nails, and the toes coming in at eight-to-ten-inches in length also having long sharp claw-like nails. When first witnessed by a gentleman driving in his car, he believed it could be a possible monkey on the loose. Another idea was a small child who was lost and scared. These theories in themselves, would not allow and explain the large glowing eyes nor the shape of the head. There are a few groups that believe this such creature to be of extraterrestrial origin. It said to roam the backroad areas and outskirts of each town. So, beware and stay focused.

━━━

ANOTHER BACKROAD DWELLER is a beast described in the seven-to-eight-foot range with red glowing eyes, and a howl that's so slow and guttural it can shake the ground. In the late evening of 2001 in the dead of summer, a man was just about to head to bed. He shut the TV off and went into the kitchen to get some water. Once he had the glass, he went over to the sink, turned the water on and let it run cool. Directly in front of the sink was a window that faced the side of his yard. You could see part of the road which is named "Nye Brook Rd." He noticed something out of the corner of his eye moving. He turned his head, focused on the object. It appeared to be a very large human crossing the road into his yard. It traveled by a clothesline that was at least six-feet-tall. The head of the being was at least a foot and a half taller. It quickly moved through the yard and into the forest. The next day the man went out and looked over the area. There was no sign of any footprints, but he did however find some broken branches high up in the area that he saw the figure enter the woods. There was no sign of what direction it went after it entered the thicket.

23

Kalamazoo County, MI
RIVER WALKER

MICHIGAN, whose capital is Lansing, achieved its statehood in 1837 and was the 26th state to join the union. Michigan is divided into two land masses known as the Lower and Upper Peninsulas. Michigan is in the center of the Great Lakes and is 96,713 square miles, with an approximate population of 9.8 million residents. The largest city in Michigan is Detroit, which is the home of the American auto industry, and holds the birth right to Motown Records founded in 1960, by Barry Gordy. According to the folks who live in Michigan, the number one food they all enjoy is the "Coney Dog." The Coney Dog to most is just a chili dog, but in Michigan it is taken to a whole new level with a variety of toppings. When done you can wash it done with a "Faygo," a soda brand that was created in the state that comes in many different flavors.

The Menominee Tribe is also part of the rich history of Michigan. The Menominee men would wear the traditional breechcloth with leggings. The women wore woven skirts, yet shirts were not a necessary part of their wardrobe. Both the men and women were known to wear mantles in the colder months. The Menominee people lived in dome shaped wigwams and rectangular styled homes. The lodges were usually covered with bark and referred to as "birch bark houses." When it came to food, the tribe was fond of wild rice which the women would harvest along with beans and squash. The men would hunt deer and would fish for Sturgeon and other kinds of fish. The men's main hunting tool was bow and arrow, and they would use spears and nets for fishing. It was always important for the people to make sure they had weapons with them, especially when near bodies of water. They would speak of a beast that they referred to as the Underground Panther. Described as a dragon, but with cougar characteristics. The tribes people feared this being and would leave offerings to appease and show respect. Some claim the creature to be flesh and blood, while others believe it to be of spirit form.

IF ONE IS A "DOG PERSON" so to speak, you might change your mind if you ever come across what the people of Michigan call the "Michigan Dogman." Dogman is said to stand seven-feet-tall and is known to attack if provoked. Some believe it to be a Werewolf, while others believe it is not a dog at all and it could be a Bigfoot. How long has this creature existed? The first reported Dogman sighting took place in 1887 in Wexford County Michigan. Dogman to some cultures of tribe's people believe the legend to be a Skinwalker type of being. Also known to some as shape shifters, like the werewolf that has the unnatural ability to transform or shape shift into the form of a wolf that walks bipedal. Many claim to have encountered the creature and barely escaped alive. Like in the theory of the werewolf, some believe that many of the human mutilation deaths are the work of a Dogman. The shear sight of the unrecognizable human body leads folks to believe there is no such animal species documented that could leave such carnage. Some remains found have been half eaten from the torso up, while others having such deep claw marks, it can be described as machete size gashes.

———

ANOTHER SUCH BEING you would not want to come face to face with is the "Kalamazoo County River Walker." Said to stand over eight-feet-tall and having red glowing eyes. In the mid-80s, a family was camping by the Kalamazoo River near the state recreation area. It was shortly after 11 pm and the family were in their tents asleep when they heard a loud splashing noise in the river. The noise sounded like it could be a large sized animal, so the father grabbed his flashlight to look and scare off whatever it was. The man told his kids to stay in their tents, and he would take care of it. He went to the edge of the river and shined the light in the direction of the noise.

What he saw, scared him to the point that he could not move. It was a Bigfoot, no doubt. It was standing in the river; the water was up to its waist. When it saw the light and the man standing on the banks, he let out a loud holler, unlike anything the man had heard before. It then turned, ran down the river against the flow with absolutely no issue. After about twenty-yards, it exited the river and made its way through an opening in the woods and disappeared. The man's family heard the holler of the beast and ran out to see what was going on. The man had them tear down the tents, pack everything up and flee the area.

24

Beltrami County, MN
HWY 25 CROSSING

MINNESOTA NICKNAMED "THE NORTHSTAR STATE," achieved its statehood in 1858 and was the 32nd state to join the union. Minnesota's state capital is St. Paul and has a population of approximately 5.3 million, with an area covering 86,935 square miles. Minnesota is the home of the Mall of America, which has more than four hundred stores, and has been said to attract over forty-million visitors a year. Along with the mall, they have some fantastic museums such as the Mill City Museum in Minneapolis, the Judy Garland Museum in Grand Rapids, and the Museum of Broadcasting in St. Louis Park.

Also, from Minnesota you will hear of the Ojibway tribe. Like other tribes, the men did the hunting, and the women performed the cooking and cleaning. Both the men and women did the farming to harvest food. The tribe was known for its artwork and music. The Ojibway people lived in village's made of birchbark houses called waginogans, also known as the wigwam. The women wore long dresses that usually consisted of removable sleeves. On their feet they wore moccasins. The men wore the traditional breechcloths with leggings. As the years passed the tribe transitioned to clothes such as blouses with jackets. They would decorate the items with various types of bead work. When the tribe went to war, they would wear head bands, with feathers standing straight up in the back. The men's hair style was a shaved head which was described as a "Mohawk," while the women had long hair which was usually braided.

The Baykok, described by the tribe's people as a creature with skeleton like features, translucent skin, and glowing red eyes. This such being is what nightmares are made of. It is said that the creature will stalk and hunt down its victims. Extremely viscous in nature, the people say it shows no remorse and will target adults and children to satisfy its evil desires and hunger.

MINNESOTA, as nice of a place as it is, has a dark being that is said to roam the land. The "Wendigo," described by some as fifteen-feet-tall and having yellow glowing eyes. Some call it the "Cannibal Giant" while others the "Maneater." It is always hungry for human flesh. It has been said the creature is of flesh and blood, while also of spirit. Legend has it, that a man once ate human flesh, and due to this he turned into the beast. Another theory is the monsters exists because of a cursed woman who dabbled in dark magic, gave birth to a baby that then turned into the Wendigo. Some believe and warn that if one comes in contact with the creature, they too can become one. The creature could possess them taking over control of the individual's body and draining its soul. Over time, the person will change from their human form, to what most describe as the most terrifying cannibalistic beast.

ANOTHER BEING to be on the lookout for is a large eight-foot-tall Bigfoot in the Beltrami County area. In 2016, a man was hitch-hiking on Highway 25 near Upper Red Lake. It was approximately 10pm. Having no luck getting a ride, he decided to take a rest and sit on a stump just off the main road. He heard a rustling noise off to his right. When he looked over, he saw a large dark figure dart out from a group of trees and run across the road. He could hear it getting further away as the trees camouflaged, and it blended into the dark. He has no idea what he saw and is not claiming it to be a Bigfoot. It happened so fast. It was there, then it was gone.

25

Lauderdale County, MS
THE YORK ROAD BEAST

MISSISSIPPI, who joined the union as the 20th state in 1817, gets its name from the "Mississippi River which is on its western border. The capital of Mississippi is Jackson and has a population of approximately three million covering an area of 48,432 square miles. During the first half of the nineteenth century, Mississippi was one of the top cotton producers in the United States. When visiting Mississippi be sure to check out some of the fantastic museums such as the Mississippi Museum of Natural Science in Jackson, or the Natchez Trace Parkway in Natchez. One place you will want to make sure you stop at would be the Jackson Zoological Park in Jackson.

Mississippi is also home to the Choctaw tribe. The Choctaw people lived in homes primarily made of plaster and rivercane walls with thatched roofs. These types of homes were strong and kept the families warm and secure as they had the strength of a log cabin. They would build their homes in a village like settings. The men wore the traditional breechcloth while the women wore wrap around skirts made of woven fabrics or deer skin. The Choctaws were famous for their artwork, rivercane baskets and wood carvings. Like all tribes, the men were responsible for the hunting while the women took care of the farming, harvesting crops of beans, squash, sunflowers, and corn.

The Choctaw people told tales of the "Kowi Anukasha" which were described as little people and would dwell hidden in the forests. It is said that they hold magical powers which they would use for good if respected. If not respected and treated or talked about poorly, they would use their magic to cast spells and curses upon anyone who dare to cross them.

IF one's passion is dance, visiting Mississippi make sure you stop in to visit Natchez Trace. The area is surrounded by beautiful forest land and can be found in the National Registry for Historic Places to visit. According to local legend, this is a haunted area that is known to the locals as "Witch Dance," a popular meeting spot for witches. When gathering in this location, the witches would perform ceremonies that included spell casting, ritual sacrifices and a ceremonial dance. It is written that wherever the witch's feet touched the ground during these dances, the grass would wither and die, never to grow again. These barren or "scorched" spots on the ground can still be seen to this day. Some individuals have witnessed what they describe as spirits twirling and circling a fire, while chanting. With no actual percussion in sight, they have described also hearing drumming coinciding with the eerie chants.

IF PASSING THROUGH LAUDERDALE COUNTY, make sure you stop at Harris Grocery off Old Highway 45 to pick up supplies. Just up the road from the store is York Road. Back in 2011, a couple of young boys were out in their back yard throwing a ball around and had a scare by what can be called "The York Road Beast." As one of the boys threw the ball, the other failed to catch it, and it went off into the woods behind him. With the tree line being outlined with thick bushes they figured they would both go and look so it did not take as long. They raced over to the area they last saw the ball rolling. As they entered the woods, they were not a bit concerned or scared as they had been in this area of their property many times. This time felt different. Usually, they can hear birds and even frogs croaking from the nearby swampy area. But it was quiet. As they stood there, they were overtaken by a horrible smell. One of the boys nudged the other while pointing to a thick area of bushes. What they described they saw, was a big ape. Standing eight-feet-tall, all black. They immediately turned, ran to their house, and told their father. When the father went into the area with his son's there was no trace of what they saw. The only thing remaining was the awful smell which as the minutes passed, it disappeared.

26

Barry County, MO
ROARING RIVER BEAST

MISSOURI, CALLED "THE SHOW ME STATE" whose capital is Jefferson City, achieved its statehood in 1821. It was the 24th state to join the union. The state is located on the Mississippi and Missouri Rivers. Its population of residents is approximately six million covering an area of 69,702 square miles. The state was an extremely important station of transportation in early American times. St. Louis, Missouri is home to Anheuser-Busch the maker of Budweiser beer which is the largest producing plant in the entire country.

The Missouri tribes people have a valuable and rich history in the state. The men are known for wearing breechcloths with leather leggings. The women wore deerskin skirts with poncho-like shirts that can also be called blouses. Both men and women were known to wear buffalo hide type robes when it became colder. During the fall and winter months, the tribe lived in settled villages of rounded earthen type lodges. The lodge type homes were made up of wooden frames covered with packed earth and branches. When hunting for food, they would look to take down big game such as buffalo and deer. Hunting, the weapon of choice was bow and arrow. When fishing they would use spears and nets. The Missouri tribe also spoke of the "Ictinike" which was believed to be a trickster spirit figure, and the son of the Son God. It has been said that this spirit, was mischievous and was always causing trouble for the tribe.

The Missouri Monster, also known as Momo, made its first appearance in the early 1970s. For weeks, this creature terrorized the community to a point that a group of hunters gathered and set out to track down and eliminate the creature. Some believed the sightings could be attributed to black bears that roam the area. But the witness descriptions say otherwise. Standing at six-to-seven-feet-tall and bi-pedal, this hairy creature is also believed to have only three toes. This claim comes from footprints witnessed by some in the area of the sightings/encounters. Some say it is a relative to Bigfoot, and others say it is a Bigfoot that has deformity of the feet. It is believed to some that the appearance of Momo can be directly linked to a rash of UFO sightings that took place in the area. Stating that the two coincide, it is believed by some that Momo could be some form of extraterrestrial being.

I believe the related sightings have to do with the creature being drawn to the energy released by the craft that has been spotted in the area. Another theory believes Momo is a paranormal entity, drawing enough energy from the space craft to manifest itself into full visual form. Some encounters consist of seeing the beast running away, while others state that the creature in fact tried to attack them. Some claim they saw the beast carrying dead animals such as deer and even pets. Regardless, it is not a being you want to come face to face with.

ANOTHER BEING you will want to avoid if possible, in Barry County, lurks in the Roaring River State Park area. Described by many as seven-feet-tall, red glowing eyes with dark brown to black matted fur. The creature has a foul odor, many attributes this to the fact that many sightings have occurred in the Roaring River Resort, in the area where they store the recycling and compost. Some say it is just a bear, but for the people who have witnessed the creature, they disagree. A couple were staying in one of the cabins with their two young children in 2014. The father could not sleep one night so he went out for a stroll around the area. He heard some noises around back in an area where the campers leave their waste and recycling. He came around the side of the building and noticed the large door that blocks the area, so it is not an eye sore to the campers was ajar. Believing a bunch of raccoons most likely were going through the trash, he shone his light in to scare them off but to his surprise there was a large shadowy figure. It was hunched over in a dumpster type container. When it stood it had to have been eight-feet-tall. Its back was to the man, and just as it was about to turn around, the man took off running to the resort's office.

Upon investigation of the area, there were signs that something had been in the containers going through the waste. They did see a couple of fleeing raccoons when they approached the area. The person the man spoke with confirmed that many have encountered the same being on different occasions. At this point, neither bear nor Bigfoot have been confirmed as the culprit.

27

Sanders County, MT
TREE BANGER

MONTANA, whose capital is Helena is the fourth largest state in the US by area just behind Alaska, California, and Texas. It has an approximate population of just under a million and covers an area of 147,039 square miles. Montana achieved its statehood in 1889 and was the 41st state to join the union. The name "Montana" comes from the Spanish Montana (mountainous), it has an elevation of only 3,400 feet. This is the lowest among the Rocky Mountains. Yellow Stone National Park is in the southern area of the state. Yellow Stone was the first park established in the United States in 1872.

Also occupying the state of Montana is the Crow Indians. The Crow men were the hunters and warriors of the tribe responsible for feeding and protecting the family. The women along with the cleaning and cooking also were responsible for building the family home and taking it apart when the family moved. The homes were tall cone shaped buffalo-hide houses. The Crow people moved a lot, so these homes were ideal. A whole village could pack up and move on in a short amount of time. The Crow men wore breechcloths, leather leggings with buckskin shirts, while the women wore long deerskin dresses.

The Crows were primarily hunting people. The men hunted elk, deer and were big buffalo hunters. The Crow Indians also harvested and grew tobacco. Some Crow warriors when protecting their families would use, war clubs, spears, shields, and bow and arrow.

There was a creature-like being the Crow tribes people spoke of that would cause chaos and were blamed for unexplained events. It was described as a troll or goblin type creature that was also referred to as the "Nirumbee." All members of the tribe were to be on the lookout for these little monsters, and to keep an eye on every child. It was believed that some disappearances of the tribes' children, could be blamed on the goblin.

Watch out for the "Thunderbird," if ever visiting. The Thunderbird has certainly made an appearance in many states, but my research brought me to Montana. The Thunderbird is a Native American legend spoken of across most to all tribes. Some tribes believe the creature to have the ability to shapeshift into human form, which allows them to communicate and live among the tribe. It was given its name due to the thunderous noise it makes while flapping its wings. Some encounters have described seeing feathers on the creature being bright in color, and in beautiful arrangement. Others have described the complete opposite, being dark and matted. With the information given, it sounds like the wingspan could be up to thirty-feet in length to create such a sound and disturbance to the human ear. It is said, the creature feasts on whales, swooping down from the sky using its large strong legs and long sharp claws to clutch, while pulling the large sea dweller out of the water. The legend of the Thunderbird is shared across the United States and Canada. There are in fact recorded sightings in other countries of similar winged cryptids.

THERE IS another beast that seems to be making a lot of noise in the state. Witnesses said the beast stands between seven-and-eight-feet-tall, and it is known to bang on trees. It is said that it hits the trees so hard it hurts the ears of the ones around him. When it hits a tree, it has been described as the same sound a car would make when colliding with another. One encounter took place with the creature in 2012 in the Sanders County area. A gentleman was fishing one early morning near the Cabinet George Reservoir just upstream. The man was sitting on a cooler listening to the sounds of the water and animal life in the area. After a few moments had passed, he noticed the woods around him went silent. It was still dark out; the sun was still a few hours from rising. He looked around but could see nothing.

Suddenly from behind he heard a loud slam sound, and pieces of wood landed all around him. He turned around and much to his surprise, there was a large dark figure standing in the eight-foot realm holding a large tree with both hands. The witness said, the figure swung the tree up against another and more pieces of wood flew in his direction. The man dropped his fishing pole and ran off. He said he never looked back, he just kept running. About six-hours later the man returned with his brothers to retrieve his pole and cooler. Where he was standing, just as he had said there were pieces of wood all around. The cooler the man had, was dumped over and the fish he had caught earlier were missing. In the surrounding area on the ground where the cooler was found, there appeared to be a partial footprint, but it could not be confirmed. The man still fishes in the same area but never alone, and always with a camera in case there is ever another encounter.

28

Dawes County, NE
CHAD

NEBRASKA, whose capital is Lincoln, was the 37th state to join the union in 1867. This was two years after the end of the American Civil War. In the 1860s Nebraska saw a large influx of settlers arriving in the state due to the 1848 California Gold Rush. At one point, the capital was Omaha but later changed to Lincoln, after President Abraham Lincoln, who had recently been assassinated. Nebraska is 77,349 square miles with a population of approximately 1.8 million. For anyone who is a fan of the drink "Kool-Aid" the beverage was invented in Hastings 1927 by Edwin Perkins. Kool-Aid is considered the official drink of Nebraska.

In Nebraska you will hear of the Omaha Indians. The Omaha men were the hunters and trappers of the family like most tribes. They mainly hunted large game such as buffalo. They were known to follow the herds to maintain a consistent diet of meat. Their choice of hunting equipment was bow and arrow and spear. If war broke out, they would fight at all costs to protect their way of life and families. The Omaha women did the cooking, cleaning, childcare, and most of the farming. The women also did most of the building and tearing down of transportable teepees the family lived in. During the colder months, the Omaha Indians lived in village type settings made up of round earthen lodge type homes. This helped to keep the family warm, safe and provide a shelter that a teepee could not offer. The women wore long skirts, while the men wore breech-cloths and leggings. The Omaha people spoke of a creature type beast they referred to as "Nida." It is said to be able to transform itself from spirit to flesh and blood. The earthly body it was believed to take on was that of an elephant. Some say the legend comes from a large set of fossils that were found that turned to flesh in front of their very eyes and became a large mammoth type of creature.

———

IF YOU'RE EVER on your way through Nebraska and heading towards Hay Springs, avoid Alkali Lake. It is said that there is a large creature living in the lake and is also responsible for eating livestock. The residents of the area call this creature "The Alkali Lake Monster" or sometimes called the "Walgren Lake Monster." Said to be anywhere from thirty-to-one-hundred-feet-long. It has had a terrifying effect on the folks who have witnessed it. Described as an alligator-type beast with a large, pointed horn on its nose, it is said to reside mostly in the water, but will come out after the sun sets to feed. There is no definitive record of humans being attacked by this bizarre creature. The legend of the Alkali Lake monster is believed by most researchers in the subject of cryptozoology to be a hoax.

———

CHADRON STATE PARK in Dawes County is home to another monster standing in the seven to eight-foot range and weighing in around seven-hundred-pounds. We'll call this one Chad for reference.

A husband and wife were hiking on the lookout trail in Chadron State Park in 2010. This seems to be a hot bed in the area for Sasquatch sightings. When the couple turned a corner, there was a large figure standing in front of them about fifty-yards away. They stopped and stared. It appeared it was the backside of whatever it was. It was in no way a bear standing on its hind legs. It was human shaped but very large and covered with what looked like black fur. The figure never turned around but left the trail and into a large area of trees. The couple, not totally sure what they just witnessed, turned the other way, and hiked back to their car. The couple has been back since the encounter hiking the same area but has not had another encounter. As much as they want to believe it was a bear, according to them, "It just couldn't be."

29

Douglas County, NV
EAGLE MOUNTAIN GIVER

NEVADA, whose state capital is Carson City which is in the western side of the country. Nevada is the seventh largest of the fifty states with an area covering 110,572 square miles with a population of approximately 2.8 million residents. The state achieved its statehood in 1864 and was the 36th state to join the union. Nevada is home of the Hoover Dam, which was the largest public works project in the history of the United States. Lake Mead, which is an attraction for tourists is the largest reservoir in the county. Gambling is legal in the state and is known around the world for its casinos and entertainment. The state is also the home of the mysterious "Area 51." This area is believed to be holding aliens and UFOs.

Also, in the state is the Washoe tribe. Known as seed gatherers and hunters. They primarily lived in the Sierra Nevada Mountain Range in small family groups. The Washoe Tribe never hunted for "sport" but always to feed and clothe their family. The people fished mostly in Lake Tahoe but also in nearby streams of water. The tribe used canoes to travel in bodies of water. They lived in camps of grass houses or temporary wikiups. The tribes' people were skilled basket weavers and created many types of baskets that used for themselves or traded for goods. The people spoke of a pleasant group of spirits that lived in the lakes and streams. They were referred to as the "Water Babies." They were described as a small spirit with magical powers. They were known to help and guide the tribe and intervene when a tribe's person was in danger.

━━

TAHOE TESSIE IS a lake monster said to dwell in Lake Tahoe. The beast first made her appearance in 1959 and has shown herself numerous times since. Like many lake creatures, her sightings have been sporadic through the decades. It is believed that Tessie is a prehistoric fish that resides and dwells at the bottom of the Lake. Some believe the fish to be female, a plesiosaur, or a prehistoric fish. Eyewitness accounts describe the large fish to be fifteen-to-twenty-feet in length and be of a dark grey color. Some encounters took place while folks were swimming in the lake. They claimed to see a large serpent creature swimming away. Others have claimed to see large grey spots in the water that upon investigation the grey spot moves and swims to the depths of the lake. The lake does in fact have sturgeon which can grow up to nine-feet in length. This could very well explain what witnesses have encountered. To date, the sturgeon theory cannot be proven as the cause. So, until science can firm, the legend of Tessie will live on.

Of course, Tessie is only one of the many monsters that reside in the state. The Eagle Mountain Giver lives in the area of Eagle Mountain. A family that lives in the area who are "off-gridders" have had multiple encounters with what they believe is the same Bigfoot. The creature is described as nine-feet-tall, brown and could weigh up to eight-hundred-pounds. The family states that they have been "gifting" with the creature for many years. Gifting is when one puts out food or an object for a Bigfoot. It is believed that when the Bigfoot comes upon it, it takes the gift and replaces it with what the Bigfoot considers to be a gift to build a relationship. This is a very common practice in the Bigfoot community of researchers and investigators.

30

Merrimack County, NH
BLACKBERRY BIGFOOT

NEW HAMPSHIRE, whose capital is Concord and is also known to some as the Granite State, achieved its statehood in 1788. It was the 9th state to join the union. With an area covering 9,348 square miles, it holds an approximate 1.3 million residents. New Hampshire was the first state to have its own constitution and the states motto is "Live Free or Die." It is also the first state to hold the national primaries. It is home to the "White Mountains." The states east coast is also known as a popular vacation destination as it hugs the Atlantic Ocean for miles and miles. One extremely popular vacation spot is Hampton Beach.

Among the many residents of New Hampshire there are also the Pennacook people. The tribe dates far back in the history of the state. The Pennacook tribe like many others lived in wigwam homes. The men were the providers of food and protection mainly using bow and arrow for hunting while using spears for fishing. The men's choice for game was deer. The women farmed while taking care of the home and children. Today some of the tribe's members still build these types of home, not for shelters but to connect with their heritage. They also will be seen wearing the traditional head bands with moccasins. The Pennacook people always kept an eye on the sky. There was always a fear of a massive bird-like creature that had a body of a serpent. It was described as having a thirty-foot wingspan and was covered in hair. The beast was said to swoop down from the skies, snatch a human, and then disappear into the sun. Not everyone witnessed this creature, but the ones who did and were lucky enough to get away, were considered to have the Sun God's blessing upon them.

———

WITH ALL THE beautiful oceanside views, one can certainly say there is a lot of water locations in the state. From the Atlantic Ocean to the myriad of lakes and ponds. There is one lake that residents talk about quite a bit, but it has nothing to do with its beauty, but more about its beast. Referred to as the "Dublin Lake Monster" by the locals, the creature has been spotted many times. It is believed that the lake has underground tunnels and passageways that would allow such a creature to exist and hide. The deepest part of the lake is said to be around one-hundred-feet, with an average depth of sixty-four-feet deep. It is approximately two hundred and forty acres. The creature, described as eel like in its appearance, and that the sight of it can put one into a state of shock and panic. The facial features of the creature according to eyewitnesses, has a shark-like rattle snake appearance. The length can be up to ten-feet-long and body as thick as a two-liter soda bottle. To this day no one has been able to get a solid clear picture of the serpent. Some believe that the Dublin Monster is a "yet-to-be" classified lake serpent.

———

LIKE BIGFOOT who also roams the state traveling under the dark of night. There have been multiple sightings in Merrimack County. Said to be a family of Sasquatch roaming the area with what is described as a male standing eight-feet-tall with brown fur, a female standing in the seven-foot range and a juvenile half their size.

Near the Black Mountain Forest region in 1998, a man was riding an ATV on a trail through the area on his way to a spot where he picks blackberries every year. While on the trail he spotted a game warden which was a problem because he was not supposed to be on the trail with an ATV, and the machine also was not registered. He quickly turned off the trail and headed in the opposite direction. Moving slowly through the woods to make as little sound as possible to not alert the possible warden, he stalled the bike. He took his helmet off and laid low. He could still see in the distance the trail and figured he would wait there until the warden passed. As he laid there still, he heard someone with heavy footsteps walking up behind him.

He quickly turned around expecting to see the same warden standing there. Much to his surprise, it was not the warden. He could not believe what he was seeing. It was a tall hairy man like creature. The body was built like an ape but had a dome shaped head and a face that was extremely human-like. Its smell could only be described as "skunk-like." The man yelled for it to get back. The beast immediately took off running and disappeared into the thick forest. The man jumped on his ATV and headed back out towards the road where he came head on with the warden. He told the warden what he had just experienced, the warden told him that the Game office received a call of a bear in the area. The warden did not believe the man's story, and as feared he was given a citation.

31

Union County, NJ
THE PINE BARRENS

NEW JERSEY, whose capital is Trenton achieved its statehood in 1787 and was the 3rd state to join the union. New Jersey has an approximate population of 8.8 million residents while covering an area of 7813 square miles. New Jersey is known to have the highest population density of all the US states. The name came from the Island of Jersey in the English Channel. Nicknamed "The Garden State," primarily due to be a leading producer in tomatoes and cranberries. New Jersey, due to its long and gorgeous coastline, has made it a popular vacation destination. There are over fifty seaside resort towns, this certainly makes it a desirable state to vacation in.

The Munsee Tribe has also made their name known in the state. The people lived in shelters like many other tribes called round houses or wigwams. This was a very commonly built home amongst tribes. The men of the tribe wore the traditional breechcloth and leggings, while the women wore knee length skirts made from woven material and deer skin. The men were the hunters of the family and equipment of choice was the bow and arrow. Their focus while hunting was on elk, turkey, and deer. When fishing they used spears and hand-woven type nets. The people were also farmers and would harvest corn, squash, and beans. The tribes people referred to these three items as the "Three Sisters." The Munsee Indians spoke of a form of little people that were described as dwarf spirits. Said to roam the land and was always playing tricks on the tribe's people. They were not dangerous and said to be benevolent, but if crossed and disrespected, they would lash out.

━━

WHEN SPEAKING OF NEW JERSEY, many will tell you about the beauty of the New Jersey Pine Barrens. If you trek out to this area just know it is also home to what the locals call the "Jersey Devil." The legend of the creature started in 1735. It is said that a woman had a curse cast upon her 13th child and she gave birth to a normal looking baby. Years later the child sprouted bat-like wings and now has a face of a cross between a horse and a goat. Another theory is the creature is a Hammerhead Bat. The Hammerhead bat is not native to the United States and resides in the tropical forest of central Africa. The theory speaks of cargo ships sailing from Africa that could have had the bats hiding on the ship, and when the journey ended and the boat docked, the bats escaped and learned to adapt to the environment. These such bats can grow to have a wingspan of up to three-feet-wide. The Jersey Devil is known to not just be seen, but to also attack at times, which would in most cases rule out the Hammerhead Bat.

Some witnesses describe the creature as looking like a combination of goat, kangaroo with bat wings. There have been more sightings of the Jersey Devil than most cryptids. The Pine Barrens are believed to be the home, but the creature is said to be nocturnal and terrorize communities at night. Law enforcement officers have even claimed to have witnessed the creature and took aim and shots at it. Parents prior to the sun going down would bring all their children in to keep them from being carried off. Pet disappearances have been blamed on the creature as well.

Cryptozoologist near and far, travel to the state to research and investigate witness encounters in an attempt to compile more information and hopefully find answers to the legend.

The Pine Barrens have a lot of stories that come out of the area pertaining to monsters and spirits, so it is not surprising to know that there are also Bigfoot sightings in the area. A couple of avid hikers were out in the Barrens enjoying the beautiful sights and calm of the area. About a mile into their hike, a stone flew across the trail in front of them. They stopped and called out to whomever threw it but received no reply. They continued determined to not let this incident hinder their experience. A few moments later another stone flew across the path in front of them. Agitated, one of the men yelled out that he had a pistol and felt threatened enough to use it. They heard nothing back, so they continued. After about 10 minutes the same thing happened, a stone was thrown across the trail in front of them. This time one of the hikers picked up a large stone and hurdled it in the direction he saw the last stone came from. It made a loud "thump" noise, and then they could hear something moving fast in the woods towards them.

They took off running and as they did, one hiker looked back to see a large figure cross the trail and head into the woods on the other side. He was the only one that witnessed this event. He stopped the other guys to inform them of what he saw. They slowly walked back to the area where the man saw the figure but found no sign of any animal or person.

32

Taos County, NM
ASPEN CREATURE

NEW MEXICO, whose capital is Santa Fe, achieved its state-hood in 1912, and was the 47th state to join the union. The state has an approximate population of 2.1 million while covering 121,590 square miles. During World War II, New Mexico was the site of the top-secret Manhattan Project, in which top US scientists raced to create the first atomic bomb. In 1947, Roswell, New Mexico, became a topic of speculation about extraterrestrial life when a local farmer discovered unidentified debris on his property. Some believed it was the remains of a crashed alien craft.

The state is also home to the Navajo Tribe. In the tribe the men were the hunters, warriors, and the political leaders. Only the men could be chiefs in the Navajo tribe. The women did the cleaning, cooking, childcare and most of the gardening. The tribes people lived in homes called hogans. A hogan is a traditional earth home. It is made of wood with packed clay. The materials made to construct such a structure helped keep the people safe from strong winds and storms. The men of the tribe wore breechcloths, while the women wore skirts made of woven yucca fibers. Both men and women wore cloaks or deer-skin ponchos. The Navajo people were considered artists of their time as they created woven rugs full of colors, turquoise and silver jewelry. They were also known for making pottery and woven baskets.

The Navajo tribe's people feared the creatures that were known to shape shift. They say the shape shifters were high ranking witches or medicine men that turned and began to use their powers for evil. It is believed that they can take on the identity of coyotes, wolves, and many other animals. The shape shifters are still to this day feared by many. Some say they tap on windows at night and can take over a human body and possess its spirit. Once the energy of the body is depleted and the soul is annihilated, it will them move on.

New Mexico is known for the infamous "Chupacabra." This creature has been seen by many and has been given the nickname of "goat sucker." Some believe the sightings to be a dog with mange. Mange is an inflammatory skin disease due to mites that can easily be spread from one dog to another. This condition can lead to hair loss, skin lesions and infections. This theory has not been proven to be fact when it comes to the Chupacabra. The Chupacabra is described as a hairless canine type of animal with a long beak like snout, with a thirst for blood. Some witnesses have described the face as canine but with reptilian features. Some detailed accounts have described long thin spike-like thorns protruding out of the creatures back.

Folks in the area keep an eye out for this creature as it has been known to attack and kill their livestock and drain its blood. The creature is suspect in all animal attacks at which the body is intact with no sign of feasting other than the carcass being completely drained of its blood. The only visual markings are puncture wounds in the neck and chest areas. Some have classified the creature as a canine vampire. The attacks are said to only happen at night. Yet eyewitnesses have in fact claimed sightings during the day. In 2008 there was a compelling video taken on a patrol cars dash camera that showed what most believe to be a Chupacabra at approximately 6:30 pm in Texas. To this day no one can confirm all the legend behind the creature, but with so many sightings and animals drained of their blood, what else could it be?

———

ALONG THE LINE of creatures of the night, there's also numerous reports of Bigfoot encounters. In Taos County a man was hunting with a friend in 2001. Both elk hunters, it was something they have done together for years. It was the early morning and the sun had not yet started to rise. Being familiar with the area and terrain the men crept quietly through the area. As they came up to a small clearing the two men saw a large figure moving along the edge of an aspen grove. It was only about eighty-feet from the two men. From what they could tell the figure had to be in the eight to nine-foot range. Being still dark, the only light showing the figure was beaming down from the moon, they could not make out any facial features. They watched as it moved back and forth near a line of trees. The two hunters agreed that one of them should shout to see what the figure does. With rifles ready to fire if needed, one of the hunters yelled out. As soon as this happened the figure turned and retreated into the woods. The hunters could hear in the distance the sound of branches breaking.

Concerned about what they had just witnessed, they stayed where they were until the sun came up. They slowly approached the area where they saw the figure. According to the height of the tree branches where its head appeared to be, they were correct with what they initially believed its size range fell into. They stood where the figure dashed into the woods and noticed broken branches extremely high up, but other than that nothing else, no trace of the creature.

33

Washington County, NY
WHITEHALL BEAST

NEW YORK, whose capital is Albany, achieved its statehood in 1788 and was the 11th state to join the union. The state has an approximate population of 19.5 million while covering an area of 54,555 square miles. It is estimated that up to forty percent of Americans can trace at least one ancestor to this port of entry. New York was also one of the states that was attacked on 9-11-2001 where the World Trade Center in New York City had two jetliners hijacked by terrorist's slam into both buildings ultimately forcing them to collapse. New York City, the largest city in the state, is home to the New York Stock Exchange which is a major international economic center.

The Oneida Tribe also resides in the state still to this day. Their history and presence in the state has been strong and contributed to what makes the state what it is today. While the men did the hunting, in this tribe the kids would often go along at a young age with their father to learn and practice the skill. Most children were not allowed in other tribes until they were in their teenage years. They would hunt for deer and turkey using bow and arrow but used a spear when fishing. The Oneida people lived in homes called longhouses. They were wooded framed buildings that were covered with sheets of elm bark. The homes could be up to one-hundred-feet-long and house up to sixty people. The men wore the traditional breech-cloths, leggings with a poncho type shirt but were not required to wear the poncho. The women wore wrap around skirts with knee high leggings with a similar type of poncho shirt which they per culture were expected to wear.

The Oneida tribe spoke of what could only be described as a living nightmare. This spirit comes in the form of a giant flying head. It has a monstrous, hideous face and would come screeching through the air at its victims. This giant disem-bodied head has been blamed for many disappearances of the tribe's people over the years. Besides this, there have been other sightings of creatures. For instance, in Upstate NY, "Georgie," the supposed beast of Lake George, has long since been admitted as a hoax. Since then, what can be described as "real" sightings have also been reported, and the possibility of a different monster in Lake George has not been put to rest or should be.

Some of these sightings have turned into old folklore, much like The Legend of Sleepy Hollow, a famous story by Wash-ington Irving. The legend takes place in the Hudson River Valley of upstate New York. The story is set at the start of the nineteenth century. Kinderhook New York is the actual Sleepy Hollow location. The town is said to have many creatures lurking the area, as well as what some call the "Kinderhook Creature," which most believe to be a Bigfoot. It is also said to have many local legends and ghost stories such as the story of Ichabod Crane, a schoolteacher who competes with Brom Bones to win over his love crush, Katrina Van Tassel. He attends a party at which he continues to seek the attention of Katrina. After the party ends, he leaves on horseback. Eventu-ally he realizes he is being stalked by what the town folks call the Headless Horsemen. Eventually after being chased by the town's feared legend, Ichabod is never seen again. All that remains of the encounter was a smashed pumpkin, in the very spot where Ichabod disappeared, never to be seen again. The legend in the area is said to be more than just a story but was in fact a true event that took place.

———

JUST NORTH OF Lake George in Washington County sits the small town of Whitehall. This location is called the Northeast "Squatch Lands" to many that research the area. Each year in September the town puts on what they call the "Sasquatch Festival." This event attracts thousands of Bigfoot fans from all over. The town is known for the famous Abair Road sighting that took place back in 1976. The reports are of three teens that were on the road just hanging out, when one of them spotted a large bipedal beast off in a field. It scared them so much that they hopped in their car and sped off and reported to the local authorities. The police responded and confirmed the sighting of the beast. Since this encounter, there has been numerous sightings in the area and encounters are still being recorded to this day. There have been so many reports that the town of Whitehall enacted a law to protect and make it illegal to harm or a kill a Bigfoot. Town officials believe, if there are Bigfoots in the area, we must protect them.

34

Cleveland County, NC
KNOBBY

NORTH CAROLINA, whose capital is Raleigh, achieved its statehood in 1789 as the 12th state to join the union. The state has an approximate population of 9.5 million and covering an area of 53,819 square miles. In 1861, North Carolina became one of the 11 states to secede from the United States beginning the American Civil War. The state in 1903 became the site of the first manned self-propelled airplane flight when the Wright Brothers took flight from a cliff near Kitty Hawk. It is also said that the evil pirate "Blackbeard" was taken out by British troops off the outer banks of North Carolina in 1718.

The Lumbee tribe has also resided in the state, and members of the tribe still do today. The name comes from the Lumber River which runs through the Lumbee homeland. Like most tribes, the men did the hunting and fishing while the women did the cleaning, cooking and most of the farming, along with taking care of the children. The men would hunt for food such as deer and wild turkeys. They would farm with their wife's vegetables such as squash, and corn. They were also known to harvest Tobacco which they would trade for other goods. The tribe is not federally recognized, this means they do not have a reservation or sovereignty rights like other tribes.

The Lumbee tribes' people have had interactions with The Little People. Described as gnome-like, the folklore of these such beings stretches across many other tribes. They have been known to make trouble and steal children's shadows, make messes so it appears the child had done it, and undo certain works that someone has completed. Some refer to them as "Boogers," which sounds like the perfect name considering their antics.

—

LAKE NORMAN to many is a place of peaceful rest and beauty. But to others, peace and beauty does not come to mind. The man-made lake is home to what the locals call the Lake Norman Monster. This such freshwater cryptid has been witnessed by many and the name has been shortened to "Normie." Prior to the creatures first sighting, it is said that the lake has extremely large fish residing in its depths. Some witnesses have claimed the fish to be as large as a small compact car. It has been confirmed that from the research I have conduct that a rare type of jellyfish has been discovered in the freshwater lake. Others have claimed seeing unusually large alligators floating the surface of the water. There is no reason alligators should be in the area according to the locals. One might ask why would this lake have so many mysteries and encounters of strange and unexplainable creatures? Many speculate it has to do with who owns the lake. Duke Energy, who runs a nuclear power plant owns the property. It is believed there has been leaks of waste from the plant that entered the lake, thus creating an atomic species of monsters.

—

ANOTHER LEGEND that is talked about and still has sightings to this day is the Bigfoot in Cleveland County. The locals refer to as "Knobby." Many folks that have witnessed Knobby claim the beast stands over seven-feet-tall. It is said the creature was nicknamed Knobby as the first sighting was seen near what is called "Carpenters Knob."

In the early 1970s a hunter in the woods claimed he saw a large bipedal monster about fifty-yards away. It did not make any noise, but just walked and disappeared into the woods. The hunter claimed the figure had gray fur from head to toe. It had a long stride with each step it took and appeared to move so smoothly that it looked like it was floating. Since this sighting, many researchers in the field of Bigfoot have searched this area. At this time, they have had unusual events but have yet had an opportunity to obtain evidence to confirm that it exists in Cleveland County.

35

Mountrail County, ND
RV BIGFOOT

NORTH DAKOTA, whose capital is Bismarck established its statehood in 1889, and was the 39th state to join the union. The state has an approximate population of 6.7 thousand, while covering an area of 70,698 square miles. Dakota is a Sioux Indian word that translates to "friend." The state became US Territory in 1803 as part of the Louisiana purchase. The region was originally part of Nebraska and Minnesota territories. The Theodore Roosevelt National Park can be found in the state along with the scenic "badlands" which is part of the park.

The Mandan Tribe who originated in North Dakota still reside there today. In the past the roles of the tribes were very traditional and very much like most tribes. The men were the hunters and fisherman of the tribes, while the women cooked and cleaned and cared for the children. The men would hunt for deer and smaller game. Their hunting equipment of choice was bow and arrow. The Mandan people lived in lodges like other tribes. When the men would leave for days to go hunting, they often took with them a buffalo-hide teepee for shelter. These were very similar in structure to how most tents are designed in the present day. The tribes people built and used bowl-shaped rafts called "bull boats" when they traveled by river. The men wore the traditional breechcloths with leggings, while the women wore long deerskin dresses. The tribes people talked lore of what they call a Mandan Coyote. The coyote was said to be powerful and like a God. The tribe considered these beings to be sacred and would look to them for wisdom, direction, and protection.

———

IN NORTH DAKOTA there is no doubt that creatures roam both the lands and waters. One creature is known as the "Devils Lake Monster." According to legend, the Devils Lake Monster is a large octopus-like beast that lurks beneath the surface of the water. Some have also described the creature as snake-like with tentacles. The creature has been described by eyewitnesses as over two-feet-wide and over sixty-feet-long. There are tales of the creature overturning boats, wrapping its tentacles around the occupants and pulling them to the bottom of the lake and devouring them.

Native Americans have claimed that they have witnessed tribe's folk in the water waist deep and then strangely pulled under the surface of the water never to be seen again. Another claim comes from a couple who were in the lake who saw a large log floating in the water. Suddenly, the log started to violently bob in the water then disappear under the surface. The couple expected to see it float back to the surface which never occurred. Something of this size could easily crush an automobile. I would avoid all lakes in this state.

———

OUTSIDE OF THE water in Mountrail County off US Highway 2 you will find a campground that a retired couple were staying at in their RV. They were enjoying their twilight years seeing the country while staying in RV parks. They had stayed at this certain RV park and packed up and headed out to continue their journey. It was early in the morning, a few minutes after exiting the park they were heading down US Highway 2. As they came up to a curve in the highway their head lights picked up movement on the side of the road. Right as the husband said, "What the hell is that?", it darted across in front of them. They hit the brakes and the RV came to a screeching stop. They looked out in the direction they saw the figure heading, but with it still dark there was no way for them to see past twenty-feet out. Shaken up, they turned the RV around and drove back to the camp. They reported what they saw to the park personnel. They described the figure as around eight-feet-tall while stating it cleared the two-lane highway in only two steps. Nothing ever came of the report, nor did they feel the park personal believed them.

36

Washington County, OH
OHIO RELATIVE

OHIO WHOSE CAPITAL IS COLUMBUS, gained its statehood in 1803 as the 17th state to join the union. It has a large population of approximately 11.5 million residents while covering an area of 44,825 square miles. Some refer to Ohio as "The Mother of Modern Presidents," having sent seven Ohio residents to the white house. In Cleveland you find the birthplace for "The Hard Rock Hall of Fame."

The Miami Tribe has also made their mark in the history of the state. Also, known as seed gatherers and hunters like the Washoe tribe. The Miami Tribe always hunted to feed and clothe their family, never for sport. They lived in small oval shaped houses with walls made of woven reeds. Each Miami village also had a large wooden council house for meetings. The tribe people were skilled basket weavers and created many types of baskets that used for themselves or traded for goods. The men wore the traditional breechcloth with leggings, while the women wore skirts with leggings along with a shirt usually decorated with a bead design. Like many creatures of lore, the Miami people had a beast they feared and spoke of often. The "Lenapizka" is a large and powerful underwater beast. The people described the creature as resembling a lynx with armor type skin. Some have described it to also have antlers like those of a deer. The creature is said to lurk in deep waters and without warning, attack and pull its victims to the depths.

———

IN THE AREA of Loveland there is a legend of humanoid amphibious creatures that are said to dwell in the area. The locals refer to these such beings as Loveland Frogmen or Loveland Lizards. Some believe there only to be one, but there has in fact been multiple sightings in different areas reported at the same time. The description from eyewitnesses confess the creature to be a large bi-pedal frog as tall as a grown man. It is also said the creature has bright glowing eyes that can be seen from a long distance away. Many photographs of the frogman have in fact shown a visual of the eyes glowing. The creatures have been even witnessed by law enforcement and it has even been said that one of the officers shot at one. The sightings since this incident have been far and few but there was another encounter in 2016 which made the news when two teen boys claimed to have come face to face with the creature. There's speculation that this sighting was a hoax played out with another teen dressing up in a supposed frog costume. Nevertheless, whether fact or faked, the legend of the Loveland Frogman lives on to this day.

———

IF ONE STUDIES the subject of Sasquatch, then without a doubt you have heard of the Ohio Grassman. This creature was first seen by the Native Americans and is described as standing over seven-feet-tall while weighing between four to five hundred pounds. Many sightings in the state are being credited to the Grassman which could very well be him or as some say, one of his relatives.

In Washington County there is a Sasquatch that also fits the description of the Grassman. In the spring of 2000, a gentleman was driving down Route 59 just outside of Cutler. He was heading west when what he thought was a deer up ahead of him about to cross the road. He saw a set of red glowing eyes, so he slowed down. As he slowly approached the figure, much to his surprise it stood up on two legs. It looked to be around eight-feet-tall with dark brown fur. The man was in shock and hit the gas. As he passed by the figure it appeared to swipe at the car. The man glanced in his rear-view mirror and witnessed the figure cross the road and disappear into the woods. The man has since driven that same stretch of road but has not had another encounter.

37

Le Flore County, OK
ROUND MIRROR BIGFOOT

OKLAHOMA, whose capital is Oklahoma City, established its statehood in 1907, and was the 46th state to join the union. It is known to some as the "Sooner State." The state has an approximate population of 3.7 million and covers 69,899 square miles. After the state joined the union, it became a center for oil production. Oklahoma did suffer from droughts and high winds which destroyed many farms and created what history calls "the Dust Bowl" of the great depression. In the 1930s it's said that over a million residents of Oklahoma moved to California due to the Dust Bowl and the "Great Depression." If one is ever planning a trip to this great state, they have a vast array of museums to visit such as, The "Science Museum," "Museum of Osteology," "American Bajo Museum," "The Oklahoma Fire Fighters Museum" and the "Oklahoma Railway Museum." They are all located in the capital, Oklahoma City.

Also in the state of Oklahoma is the Quapaw tribe. They have a long history in the state. The tribe had its own government, laws, services, and police. This did not allow them to disobey the laws of America as they were considered US citizens. The men of the tribe would hunt every day for food, which was usually deer and small game using bow and arrow. They would also fish using spears. The women took care of the cooking, cleaning, and childcare. Both the men and women took part in the farming and harvesting crops of beans, squash, and corn. The Quapaw people lived in square houses made of plaster and rivercane walls with thatched roofs. The men wore breechcloths, leather leggings with buckskin shirts, while the women wore deerskin dresses. Both men and women wore moccasins. The women wore their hair braided or loose while the men would shave their heads except for a section that they referred to as a "Scalp lock." This was one long lock of hair on the back of their heads. The tribes people spoke of the "Pahi Zka Jika," which was said to be a troll like spirit. Mischievous and fast, the troll would play tricks on the people and even hide some of the tribe's belongings. Some have claimed the spirit could become dangerous if upset, but most claims reported them to be peaceful and pleasant.

ALLIGATOR MAN? Yes, Oklahoma is known for the legend of the Alligator Man. The first sighting with validity recorded took place in the early 1920s. The Alligator Man has been described as having a human body but with an alligator's head. This strange creature and any claims have had a lot of scrutiny and push back regarding the existence. In most cases when a creature is first witnessed, it will usually follow with others coming forward, or other encounters in the same time frame. In regard to the Alligator Man, from my studies and research, this isn't the case. Regardless, such a creature existing to a certain fisherman who claimed an encounter believes. The individual wasn't overly forth coming with details but did state his life hasn't been the same.

ANOTHER CREATURE that is worth talking about stands over seven-feet-tall and has been seen roaming the Le Flore County area. In the early months of 2006 in the Big Cedar area off Route 259, a woman was riding a motorcycle and pulled over to take a break and stretch her legs. While resting she noticed a secondary dirt road that went into the wooded area. She hopped back on the bike and started down the road. She was enjoying the beauty of the area when in one of her round mirrors she saw what she described as a large ape-like creature chasing after her. It frightened her to the point where she froze up, and the bike started to slow down. She could see the figure getting closer and closer. She snapped out of the fear, sped up and watched the figure get further and further away. The next opening off the road, she took and sped away. She told her husband about the encounter who believes it was a person playing a prank. Either way, she has decided she will never go on that road or near that area again.

38

Clackamas County, OR
OREGON LEDGE JUMPER

OREGON, whose capital is Salem achieved its statehood in 1859 as the 33rd state to join the union and is the 9th largest state in the US. Oregon covers an area of 98,379 square miles and has an approximate population of 3.8 million residents. In the 1930s many groups of pioneers traveled to the state on the Oregon Trail. In 1846, the border between the US and British territories was formally established at the 49th parallel. The portion that was given to Britain in the end became a part of Canada.

Also, in Oregon you will find the Klamath tribe. The tribe's people can still be found today in the state. In the past the tribes people lived in earth type lodges. The shelters were cone-shaped frame of wooden poles placed over what can be described as a basement type hole dug in the ground. The frame was covered with brush and packed with a mound of earth to help keep it insulated. The men wore short wrap-around kilts made of deerskin with a deerskin poncho type shirt depending on the weather. The women wore long skirts made of buckskin and decorated with beads. The Klamath people were known to wear both moccasins and a sandal type shoe. The men did the hunting of deer, small game, and the fishing, while the women did the farming, cleaning, and child-care. The Klamath people like many other tribes, spoke of and feared a dragon type water serpent. The lore behind this crea-ture is believed to have begun when a curse was cast onto certain bodies of water in the area. The curse is said to have been placed by a rival group of rebellious natives that were so evil in their ways, they were granted special powers from past evil witch's and medicine men. It is believed, some of these evil spirits possessed these individuals and are using them to bring chaos to the land.

IF YOU'RE familiar with the Columbia River in Oregon and would like to visit to see its beauty, just be careful and keep an eye out for what the locals call "Colossal Claude." Claude first made his appearance in the 1930s at the mouth of the Columbia River. Witnesses say this river serpent is between forty and fifty-feet-long and has a long neck that can rise out of the water. Some encounters with the serpent have been said to be of violent in nature. Years back I had heard of an encounter at which the beast was said to have flipped a canoe over and attempted to drown the occupant of the small river craft. The young man fought and was able to make it to land. The creature was described as dark black and its skin was extremely slippery, which allowed the young man to escape its grip. Another encounter claims the creature swam by and knocked a person off their feet. The individual fell and was submerged under the water. They stood up and was able to quickly retreat to land. At this point, the locals choose to stay on land and out of the river to avoid any contact with Claude.

IN CLACKAMAS COUNTY, it is on land where you will have to watch your back. In the early 2000s, a research team in the field of Bigfoot was searching a local area that had many reports. While they entered this one area, out on a mountains ledge they could see a large figure making its way very easily across the dangerous landscape. It was about five-hundred-yards away. They watched as the figure effortlessly jumped from ledge to ledge. Soon the figure entered an area and was no longer in sight. The team made their way over to the location they witnessed the figure but were unable to locate any type of footprints or hair. They could, however, confidently say it had to be in the eight-foot range. Also, the area where the ledges had openings from one ledge to the next were approximately ten-feet apart. This would appear to be out of a human range due to the ground being unleveled with no real way to get a running start. At this point it cannot be confirmed or denied as a Sasquatch sighting.

39

Fulton County, PA
THE COWAN'S STATE PARK SIGHTING

PENNSYLVANIA, whose capital is Harrisburg, achieved its statehood in 1787 as the 2nd state to join the union. The state has a large population that is approximately 12.8 million while covering 46,055 square miles. Its largest city is Philadelphia. As one of the original thirteen colonies, Pennsylvania was founded by William Penn, and was a haven for his fellow Quakers. In the American Civil War 1861-1865, the state was the site of the battle of Gettysburg and Lincoln's famous Gettysburg address. The state also has a vast amount of unique and fascinating museums one can visit such as, the Mutter Museum in Philadelphia, The Harry Houdini Museum in Scranton, The Liberty Bell Museum in Allentown, and The Living Dead Museum in Evan City.

Also heralding from the state of PA are the Conestoga Indians. The people were an Iroquoian tribe of Pennsylvania and Maryland. The tribe suffered many losses from disease and warfare. The men wore the traditional breechcloths with leggings. The women wore a wraparound skirt with deerskin shirts. The men were the hunters, as they hunted deer and small game. They also took care of all the fishing. The women took care of the children, cleaned, and did the farming. The Susquehannock Indians and Conestoga Indians are related to each other. The Conestoga spoke of and feared, the same creature. They told stories of a wild and hairy cannibalistic creature that roamed the lands. Said to be eight to nine-feet in height, with a slender build. The tribes people still speak of this creature's lore today, but many believe it was just a Sasquatch.

———

THE HAYCOCK MOUNTAINS also know as the "Ghost Mountains," there is a legend of the "Albino Cannibals." Legend has it, that these creatures are an inbred race of people who like vampires have a lusting thirst for blood. It is said they chase cars, ambush hunters and hikers. Once they have their hands on you, no one ever hears from you again. Some compare this legend to the Hollywood horror film "The Hills Have Eyes." The locals of the Sellersville area speak of this lore. These such cannibals are said to be nocturnal only emerging at night. They live their lives hidden in the deep woods where they have the advantage. It is believed that they will purposely construct and lay out rocks and trees on backroads to prevent folks from trespassing then lure them out of their vehicle so they can capture them and feast on their flesh.

It is believed that they live underground in cave-like hideouts. Some believe they are made up of concrete which helps muffle the screams of the victims while they devour them. It is also believed that the Albino Cannibals are not just to blame for the disappearance of humans, but also livestock. The farmers believe they come by night and raid their property stealing anything from chickens to larger stock such as goats and sheep. The shear fear of encountering one keeps the locals in at night behind locked doors and windows, as to avoid becoming victim to an Albino Cannibal.

━━

IN THE AREA of Fulton County, a creature has been seen by many in the Cowan's State Park area. In 2005 four friends went on a hike. About sixty-minutes in, one of the hikers started to feel dizzy. They stopped, took a water break, and had a snack. The thought was this was just what the hiker needed. They sat for about ten-minutes while the dizziness seemed to dissipate. They continued for a few minutes until the same hiker that experienced being dizzy mentioned that his head was now pounding. They sat and took another break. A few minutes later one of the other hikers seemed extremely nervous and wanted to turn back. They all agreed that this was the best plan, as they started to get extremely concerned about their friend's well-being.

As they headed back, one of the hikers saw what looked like a large man in a ghillie suit standing behind a tree. The figure looked to be around seven-feet-tall and seemed to sway back and forth. Curious about what he might be seeing, he turned and mentioned it to the group. They all turned, looked in the same direction. As they did the figure moved back and did not show itself again. Concerned about what they just saw and the health of their friend, they continued back to the cars. When they arrived in the parking area, the man who was under the weather seemed to be doing better. To this day they are not sure what they saw behind the tree.

40

Washington County, RI
LOVERS NIGHTMARE

RHODE ISLAND, whose capital is Providence, established its statehood in 1790, and was the 13th state to join the union. The state was founded by Roger Williams in 1636. To date the name "Rhode Island" is of uncertain origin. The state is also known to some as "The Ocean State" but has many other nicknames such as Southern Gateway to New England and Little Rhody. The state is one of the smallest in the country at only 1,545 square miles but has a large population of approximately 1.1 million residents. If ever in the state you can visit the Tennis Hall of Fame, the Providence Children's Museum, the Newport Car Museum, or the Newport Art Museum.

The state of Rhode Island is and has been for a long time, the home of the Nipmuc tribe. The tribe spoke a language of the Narragansett tribe, but the language went away more than one-hundred years ago. Some members today are making it a point to revive it for history to continue the culture. Like most tribes, the men were the hunters and focused on deer and small game and took care of the fishing. Their choice of hunting equipment was bow and arrow, and spears when fishing. The women took care of the cleaning, cooking and childcare. Some say the tribes people lived in teepees, but also lived-in wigwams like the Pequot Indians. The men wore breechcloths with leggings, while the women wore knee-length skirts. Along with hunting and fishing, the Nipmuc people were farmers and harvested corn, beans, and squash. The people feared and spoke of the "Hobomock" also referred to as the "Spirit of Death." This spirit is said to create chaos among the people, and even possess the tribe's folk at times. The spirit is said to be so evil; it is often compared to the devil of the bible.

AS WE SPEAK of residents in the state, we should also mention the Block Island Monster. In 1996 a bizarre creature was pulled up in a fishing net. The creature had passed through many phases of physical decomposition and decay. The locals were not sure what to make of the creature. Folks came from all around to witness this unexplainable sight. One day, the creature's carcass disappeared. It is believed by some that government officials had taken the body as to hide the existence, while others believe the towns people took it and hid it to preserve and respect the creature. There was a lot of speculation on what it could be. A New York State biologist traveled out to examine the carcass prior to the disappearance, and it is said he was baffled and was unsure of what he was looking at. Ultimately in the end it is believed that it was a dead basking shark. Not everyone is convinced with this conclusion.

THERE IS another story of a creature that calls the state home that is described as standing seven-feet-tall with huge shoulders, a dome shaped head and has an extremely loud grunt. In 1975 in Washington County, a young adult couple were staying overnight in the Great Swamp Management Area. They were staying in the back of their pickup truck that was sheltered with a bed cab. As the couple slept, the woman was awakened with an awkward feeling that they were being watched. She sat up and looked out one of the windows but saw nothing. She laid back down, was almost a sleep when she heard a grunting noise. She laid there for a minute and heard it again, but this time it was louder. She sat up and as she looked out the window, she saw a large figure walking by. She quickly woke the man up and told him what she just witnessed. He attempted to get out to look, but the woman would not let him leave her. They sat the rest of the night watching and listening, but whatever the woman saw never came back. The man to this day believes she was sleeping and dreamt the whole encounter. The woman on the other hand said she knows what she saw, and she certainly was wide awake.

41

Sumter County, SC
SUMTER ENCOUNTER

SOUTH CAROLINA, whose capital is Columbia established its statehood in 1788 and was the 8th state to the join the union. The state was settled by the English in the year 1670. It has an approximate population of 4.7 million residents while covering an area of 32,021 square miles. The state borders North Carolina, Tennessee, and Georgia. It has a beautiful coastline touching the Atlantic Ocean. Myrtle Beach on the coastline has become a premiere resort destination on the East Coast. There are also over one hundred golf courses in the state.

In South Carolina you will find the Catawba tribe. The tribe's people can still be found today in the state. In the past, the tribes people lived in earth type lodges. The shelters were cone-shaped frames of wooden poles. The frame was covered with brush and packed with a mound of earth with bark walls to help keep it insulated. The men wore short wraparound kilts made of deerskin with a deerskin poncho type shirt depending on the weather. The women wore long skirts made of buckskin and decorated with beads. The Catawba people were known to wear a moccasins type shoe. The men did the hunting of deer, small game, and the fishing, while the women did the farming, cleaning, and childcare. The Catawba people like the tribes in relation to them, believed in mischievous dwarf spirits. They are said to play tricks on the tribe's people and could sometimes be extremely destructive to the people's homes and belongings. Stories of the spirits were told to the children to keep them in line, and in their beds at night.

———

I WAS ONCE TOLD of a legend that comes from South Carolina. For many of the people from the state, the legend is not just surrounded by myth and stories, but of facts and occurrences. First spoken about by the Gullah people, the legend gives way to the knowledge of the "Boo Hags." They are described as a vampire-witch type being that can appear as spirit and even on occasion in flesh form. It is believed the Hags will make their way into one's home via open windows or even small cracks in the foundation. It is said once it enters, it will not drain you of blood like most vampire legends but suck the life out of your lungs while sitting on your chest. One description claims the Hags will ride the body to exhaustion draining just the energy. Other claims state they will slip into your skin and use your body to move about through the night. It is believed when one wakes up in the middle of the night and cannot move their body, they have sleep paralysis as defined by modern medicine. The people of South Carolina will tell you different. They believe the Hags to be real, and fear closing their eyes at night.

———

THERE IS another creature in the state that moves about the night in Sumter County. Described as a large seven-foot-tall ape creature with brown fur and a menacing holler. In 2006, several friends were hunting in a patch of woods that was registered as legal hunting ground. They were each in their own deer stands when they heard a strange sounding "bellowing" holler. Being hunters their whole lives, they were familiar with the sounds of the woods, and the wildlife that called the area home. They looked at each other, they all had the same confused expression. That is when they saw a large, dark colored creature, standing about fifty-yards away. The creature noticed one of the hunters and let out a menacing holler. It was so loud, one of the hunters shot his rifle to scare off the creature, which seemed to work. The beast hurried off and disappeared into the thick woods. After a few moments, the hunters all gathered on the ground to discuss what they had just witnessed. They slowly made their way over to where the creature was standing and found a large footprint. They documented while taking pictures of the print, and the surrounding area. They have gone back to the same spot many times but have yet to have another encounter. However, they have experienced in the distance, a similar vocal. At this time, it cannot be confirmed, that it was, in fact from the beast they witnessed.

42

Todd County, SD
ROSEBUD SASQUATCH

SOUTH DAKOTA, whose capital is Pierre, was awarded its statehood in 1889 as part of the Louisiana Purchase, and became the 40th state to join the union. With an approximate population of eight hundred and fifty-thousand and covering an area of 77,116 square miles. In the present day, a major part of South Dakota's economy is due in part by tourists who flock to the state to see such locations as Mt. Rushmore which features sixty-foot-tall sculptures of four past presidents. This sculpture includes Washington, Jefferson, Roosevelt, and Lincoln. Along with famous presidents carved in stone, you would be intrigued to know that Ranae Holland was born in South Dakota in 1970. From Sioux Falls, Ranae was one of the members of the popular TV show, *Finding Bigfoot* that aired on the Animal Planet from 2011 to 2018. Ranae first refused to join the team as she is a skeptic of Bigfoot's existence. She did however grow up with a father who had a fascination with the legend of the creature.

South Dakota is also known for the Arikara Tribe. The Arikara men were hunters and would sometimes go to war in the event they needed to protect their families and loved ones.

The women were farmers while doing most of the cleaning and took care of the children. They lived in shelters known as lodges which were constructed with wooden type frames and were covered usually using branches with packed earth like material. The homes were usually larger than what most other tribes would construct due to the fact they preferred all family members live in the same home. Some homes could be as large as fifty-feet across. The Arikara women wore wraparound skirts with deerskin type shawls. The men wore leather leggings, breechcloths, and buckskin shirts. The tribe would hunt deer, buffalo as well as small game. The bow and arrow were their choice when hunting or going to war. Chirich, would be what the tribe would call a "trickster figure." Described as a coyote, and for some reason purposely getting in the peoples way and setting them up for failure or criticism in certain situations involving tribe morals. It is believed they are known to live the full life cycle of a coyote, but once the body dies, the spirit leaves, only to return giving the body new life.

IN THE DESERT area of the state there is a spirit type being called the "Banshee of the Bad Lands." It is said that the cries are so hideous that one's blood could grow cold just at the sound. Some have claimed that the sound is so ear piercing, many have lost the ability to hear or now have permanent ringing in their ears. This being has been described as having long flowing hair, and the arms waving in unknown gestures that are terrifying to witness. The spirit has been reported to be standing on the ground screaming in hysteria, while other reports claim witnessing her floating through the air.

There seems to be no warning prior to the spirit showing up. The legend in the state of the banshee tells of an Indian woman who had been murdered by a jealous lover. Now she wonders in deep pain and distress in this desolate area of the state. Irish folklore speaks of the banshee as a spirit that will be heard screaming which is significant, as this occurrence is said to follow with a death of a family member. A frightening and spine-tingling tale to say the least.

———

THERE IS ALSO another terrifying being roaming South Dakota. Described as a large black animal-like man, there has been multiple sightings especially in Todd County. In the area of the Rosebud Indian reservation in Todd County, a young woman had a roadside encounter. Taking place on a secondary road just off Route 83, the woman was on her way home from picking up her children from her parents. It was in the early morning as the she worked the night shift a local retail outlet. As she drove down the road, her oldest child started yelling "bear."

The woman looked in the direction the child was pointing and witnessed a large black animal on all fours. It was far enough away that she slowed down to let her children watch it for a few minutes. As they watched, the child pressed the window button lowering the window and yelled out. Much to her surprise, what she thought was a bear hunched down, stood straight up, turned, and looked at them. The woman was terrified. The creature let out a loud roar and waved its arms which were long and dropped down near its knees. The woman hit the gas and sped away. The whole way home the children kept asking why they could not continue to watch the bear. The woman arrived at home and allegedly notified the authorities of what she had witnessed. In her opinion, it was in no way a bear, but had to be a Bigfoot.

43

Sullivan County, TN
HOLSTON LAKE FIGURE

TENNESSEE ACHIEVED its statehood in 1796 and was the 16th state to join the union. Its capital is Nashville and has an approximate population of 6.5 million residents, while covering an area of 42,144 square miles. The state is just one hundred and twelve miles wide but stretches four hundred and thirty-two miles from east to west. The state's two largest cities are Nashville and Memphis. The two cities are known as the heartland of blues county music. When one thinks of BBQ, Memphis will surely come to mind as they host a large BBQ competition event each year.

Residing in the state is the Chickasaw tribe. The men of the tribe would hunt every day for food which was usually deer and small game using bow and arrow. They would also fish using spears. The women took care of the cooking, cleaning, and childcare. Both the men and women took part in the farming and harvesting crops of beans, squash, and corn. The Chickasaw people lived in square houses made from plaster, and rivercane walls with thatched roofs. The men wore breechcloths, leather leggings with buckskin shirts, while the women wore deerskin dresses. Both men and women wore moccasins.

The tribe's people were known for their woodcarvings and artistic pottery. The Chickasaw tribe believed in the "Sint-Holo," which is described as a dragon-like serpent. The Sint-Holo also has a snake type face with a horn protruding out of the top of its head. Some believed it was a spirit let loose upon them as a curse for immoral behavior. While others believed it to be a flesh and blood creature, which roamed the land.

THE STATE HOLDS a massive number of monster and unknown creature sightings. One such creature is the Tennessee Wildman. Legend has it, in the 1800s a freak showman captured the beast from unknown parts and while traveling through the state it broke free and has eluded capture since. It has been described as looking "Sasquatch-like." Said to be in the seven-foot range in height, with dark fur-like hair. The Wildman is said to be very human-like and less animal. It possesses the ability to be able to move and run at a high rate of speed. The eyes are described as piercing red. The vocal of the Wildman is described as high pitch and piercing to the ear. It is said that he is extremely violent in its behavior as its extremely territorial. It is believed the Wildman has an appetite for and will target dogs, cats, and livestock as meals. Believed by some that the Wildman has since passed but has spawned offspring that carries the same traits and is why as of today, there are still reported sightings.

One such sighting took place in Sullivan County near Holston Lake in 2009. Some friends were at the end of Friend-ship Road hanging out and just talking. It was mid-afternoon, and extremely hot out. They decided to venture through the forest to the nearby lake. Once they arrived at the lakes edge, they noticed a smell that was extremely skunk-like, it made their eye's water. Not overly concerned about running into a skunk, they made their way into the lake. As they submerged their bodies in the water and cooled off, one of the folks noticed movement up in the wooded area near where they left their shirts and shoes. Concerned that some of them had their wallets in their shoes, they hurried out of the water and stood by their belongings. They could still see a figure lurking in the wooded area near a tree. The skunk smell seemed stronger than earlier. One of the swimmers yelled out asking if the figure needed help. There was no reply.

Another one yelled out while flinging a rock in the direction of the figure. Once the rock landed, the figure stepped out in plain view and let out a roar. They could not believe what they were seeing. The creature was in the eight-foot range and had to be at least six-hundred-pounds. It turned, ran off into a thick wooded area and vanished. The group stood there in shock, then grabbed their belongings, and ran back to their cars. In their minds they know what they witnessed. To this day they have not returned to that area of the lake again.

44

Bexar County, TX

BEXAR BIGFOOT

TEXAS, also called the Lone Star State, achieved its statehood in 1845, and was the 28th state to join the union. The states capital is Austin and has an estimated population of 25.5 million residents, while covering an area of 268,597 square miles. History tells us that Spanish missionaries were the first European settlers in Texas founding San Antonio in 1718. The state has a vast variety of history and science museums that are a must to visit if you're ever in the state.

The Comanche Tribe can also be found in Texas. In the past the roles of the people were very traditional and much like most tribes. The men were the hunters and fisherman of the tribes while the women cooked and cleaned while caring for the children. The men would hunt for deer and smaller game. Their hunting equipment of choice was bow and arrow. The Comanche people lived in lodges like many other tribes. When the men would leave for days to go hunting, they often took with them a buffalo-hide teepee for shelter. These were very similar in structure to how most tents are designed in this present day. The Comanche Indians were not coastal people and rarely traveled by river. One type of transportation used were "travois" a dog sled like boat that was pulled by dogs to get around. The people were known to trade with other tribes in the Southwest. It is written that the trade of horses was their focus and they are responsible for the rapid spread of breeds throughout Western America.

The Comanche tribe's people like the Navajo tribe feared the Skinwalkers. They say the Skinwalkers were high ranking witches or medicine men that turned and began to use their powers for evil. Also known as shape shifters, it is believed that they can take on the identity of coyotes, wolves, and many other animals. The Skinwalkers are still to this day feared by many. Some say they tap on windows at night and can take over a human body and possess its spirit. Once the energy of the body is depleted and the soul is annihilated, it will them move on.

THERE IS a legend in Texas that has become the talk of the state, if you will. There has been reports of a large bird called by the locals "Big Bird." The creature is described as a large, winged beast with an ape-like face. It is said that it first made its presence known in 1976 in South Texas. Since its first sighting, there has been multiple witness encounters throughout the area, even by a police officer who claims he saw the creature in the headlights of his cruiser. There was another encounter that took place involving two teenagers. They described the creature as standing in the five-to-six-foot range. It was like nothing they had ever witnessed. The man-sized bird continued making appearances with witnesses describing the wingspan to be over twelve-feet from wing tip, to wing tip, and having three toes.

There have also been a few reports of the giant bird attacking humans. They are far and few, but nevertheless, just one claimed attacked is enough to put the locals of the state in a well understood panic. There are still reported sightings of large, winged bird creatures in the state, but the lore and unexplainable creatures are now witnessed across the country.

———

IN THE AREA of Bexar County there is another cryptid that is surely making a name for itself. Described as brown in color, having a horrible stench, and standing between seven and eight-feet-tall is the Bexar Bigfoot. Most of the sightings have taken place in the Government Canyon State Natural Park. Sightings date back to the early 1970s.

The Government Canyon State Natural Park is known for its hiking trails and beautiful surroundings. In the mid 1990s a woman took her dog for a walk on one of the trails. This was a weekly routine that the woman enjoyed, as she was able to get away from the hustle and bustle and just connect with nature. About thirty-minutes into the walk her dog stopped and would not move. This was unusual behavior. She tried to coax him on, but he would not go any further. He started to back up and seemed to want to turn around and go the other direction. The woman began to be concerned about the dog thinking he might be ill. She gave in and started to head back the way they came.

As they started down the trail, the woman heard a noise of a stick breaking behind her. She turned and looked, off to the side of the trail stood a large hairy figure. She screamed at the sight, turned, and ran. As she continued to run in the opposite direction, she came upon a few other hikers. She communicated what she had just witnessed and was in total panic. The hikers walked back to the parking area alongside her. Asking if it could have been a bear or someone playing a prank. The woman knows what she had witnessed, and to this day has never returned to what was once her favorite place to be.

45

Cache County, UT
CANYON VIEW SIGHTING

UTAH, ALSO CALLED THE "BEEHIVE STATE" by some established its statehood in 1896 and was the 45th state to join the union. The capital of the state is Salt Lake City with an approximate population of 2.8 million and it covers 84,897 square miles. Utah is known to have the best skiing in the country due to the mountains in the area averaging over five-hundred-inches of snow per year. In the nineteenth century many Mormons moved into Utah. As of today, over sixty percent of the state's residents are members of the Mormon church. Each January in Park City the state holds "The Sundance Film Festival" which is one of the premiere independent film festivals in the world. Utah's Great Salt Lake is the largest saltwater lake in the western hemisphere. Utah is also home to the Skinwalker Ranch which has gained national attention over the years.

Utah is also home of the Ute Tribe. The Ute men were hunters and would sometimes go to war in the event they needed to protect their families and loved ones. The women were farmers while performing most of the cleaning and took care of the Ute children. They lived in shelters known as "lodges" which were constructed with wooden type frames and were covered usually using branches with packed earth like material. The homes were usually larger than what most other tribes would construct due to the fact they preferred all family members live in the same home as the Kansa tribe highlighted in earlier chapters. The Ute women wore wraparound skirts with deerskin type shawls. The men wore leather leggings, breechcloths with buckskin shirts. The tribe would hunt deer, buffalo as well as small game. The bow and arrow were their choice when hunting.

The Ute tribe like the Navajo people believed there were wolves that could turn human, also believed to be Skinwalkers or Shapeshifters. These were not seen as werewolves, but simply a cursed human, that now walks most of its days on all fours. Others believe it is a human, which can turn into a wolf. The word "wolf," is considered to translate as "man." This is said to come from the tribe's formal language. It is also believed the Skinwalkers could have been high ranking witches or medicine men that turned and began to use their powers for evil. The Skinwalkers are still to this day feared by many. Some say they tap on windows at night and can take over a human body and possess its spirit. Once the energy of the body is depleted and the soul is annihilated, it will then move on. They are also suspected to be involved in the numerous unexplained livestock and cattle mutilations that occur in the state each year.

UTAH IS no stranger to folklore tales and legends of monsters and creatures. One legend revolves around Bear Lake. The monster has been named the "Bear Lake Monster." It is described as a snake-like creature with a serpent type head and a large mouth. Its slithering body is said to be ninety-feet-long, and brown in color. The native Americans in the area have told tales of the creature capturing and carrying away people.

The Beaver Mountain Ski Area in Cache County is home of a sighting by a couple of friends who were snowboarding. The sighting took place in 2017 on the Canyon View trail. As the three friends were boarding down the mountain, they were on the edge of the Canyon View trail when they noticed a large black figure standing by a tree. All three saw the figure as it was only about fifty-yards away. As they slowed down to get a better look, the figure turned and ran off into the distance. The snow was waist deep but to the creature it was only to its knees. When it turned and ran off, it plowed through the deep snow with ease which would not be possible for a regular human. They hurried down the mountain and upon reaching the bottom of the trail, they reported what they witnessed to staff members of the resort. They arranged to have someone check the area which did in fact show something large had been there and slammed through the snow.

46

Orleans County, VT
INTERSECTION ENCOUNTER

VERMONT WHOSE CAPITAL IS MONTPELIER, established its statehood in 1791, and became the 14th state to join the union. The state has an approximate population of six-hundred-and-fifty-thousand, while covering an area of 9,616 square miles. Vermont was initially settled in the early eighteenth century by both the British and French. The name of the state comes from "montagne verte" which is French for green mountains. This is how the state received their nickname, "The Green Mountain State." The state is popular for its skiing and snowboarding. Vermont is also known for its maple syrup. Vermont's famous maple syrup is made from sap from the sugar maple in the state tree. The state is the largest producer of syrup in the United States. Approximately seventy-five percent of the state's land is forest.

The Abenaki Tribe has also made their name known in the state. The people lived in shelters like many other tribes called round houses or wigwams. This was a very commonly built home amongst tribes. The men of the tribe wore the traditional breechcloth with leggings, while the women wore knee length skirts made from woven material and deer skin. The men were the hunters of the family and their equipment of choice was the bow and arrow. Their focus when hunting was on elk, turkey, and deer. When fishing they used spears and hand-woven type nets. The people were also farmers who would harvest corn, squash, and beans. The Abenaki people spoke of the "N-dam-keno-wet," which is described as a half fish, and half man. Most creatures of this type are found in the oceans of the world, and considered to be a Mermaid or Mer-Man. The major difference is this creature can be found in lakes and streams. In most cases, this type of creature is said to be flesh and blood, but for the Abenaki it is a water spirit.

VERMONT IS a beautiful place to visit especially the city of Burlington. The city also has a great view of Lake Champlain, a freshwater lake that borders both New York and Vermont. The deepest section of the lake is over four-hundred-feet, which would allow enough room for "Champ," the Lake Champlain Monster to exist. Described as a long serpentine type of creature, some have compared its features to The Loch Ness Monster, who resides in Scotland. The first sighting of the creature dates to the 1800s. As of the present day there are still reported sightings. Many have managed to take a photo of Champ.

The Mansi Photograph which to this day is considered to be the most intriguing photo taken of Champ. In 1977 Sandra Mansi was on the shores of Lake Champlain when she saw what she believed to be a lake monster surface from the depths of the water. She grabbed her camera and took the picture that is now considered to Champ enthusiasts, what the Patterson Gimlin footage is to the Bigfoot community. To this day like the Patterson Gimlin film, this photo has not been debunked. The validity of the photo is still debated and analyzed to this day, with the same ending conclusion, it is real.

━━

IF THERE IS a sea creature lurking in Vermont, we know there will certainly also be some Sasquatches as well. There have been stories and sightings of seven-to-eight-foot-tall creatures hiding in the forested areas of the state. In Orleans County in the mid 2000s, a man and his girlfriend had a sighting as they were driving south on Vincent Road. It was just after 11pm and they were heading home from a night out with some friends. It was just before Christmas, and was an extremely cold night, and lightly snowing. As the couple came to an intersection, they were just about to turn onto Veilleux Road when a large bi-pedal figure stood up on the roads edge directly across from them.

They were no more than ten-feet from the figure, and with the headlights directly on the being, they could immediately tell this was not a person. It stood around eight-feet-tall, was all black, and had massive red eye shine. It raised its arm to block the lights that were beaming directly at it. It then turned and ran into the forested area directly behind it. The couple just sat there amazed at what they just witnessed. They at first, were very forth coming and talked about the encounter, but gone quiet as they received a lot of backlash and ridicule.

47

Botetourt County, VA
GRUNTING AND SNARLING

VIRGINIA, whose Capital is Richmond, established its statehood in 1788, and was the 10th state to join the union. The state has an approximate population of 8.2 million while covering an area of 42,775 square miles. The state was also home to four of the first five presidents, George Washington, Thomas Jefferson, James Madison, and James Monroe. Today there are many government institutions headquartered in the state. The state also has a few nicknames such as "The Old Dominion," "Mother of States," "The Cavalier State" and "Mother of Presidents." It also has its share of slogans such as "Where Love Lives," "Live Passionately" and the most popular "Virginia is for Lovers." With all their nicknames and slogans, they also have some great museums like "The Virginia Museum of Fine Arts," "Military Aviation Museum" and the "Whitehouse of the Confederacy."

The Croatoan tribe also resides in the state, first migrating north from North Carolina, and is related to the Algonquian tribe. Like most tribes the men did the hunting and fishing, while the women did the cleaning, cooking and most of the farming along with taking care of the children. The men would hunt for food such as deer and wild turkeys. They would farm with their wives for vegetables such as squash and corn. They were also known to harvest tobacco, which they would trade. The people of the tribes feared the same beast as the Algonquian Indians. This creature is a mythical flying beast. Described as a flying snake-like serpent with a wide wingspan. The creature has been said to ambush its prey from above and carry it away. Young children were said to be the most to fall victim of this monster.

THE SHEEPSQUATCH HAS BEEN sighted numerous times in the state. Eyewitnesses have described the visual appearance of the Sheepsquatch as a large grizzly bear that is bipedal and walks on its hind-legs. The feet on the creature are said to be hoofs as you would find on a sheep. The body is covered with sheep-like fur that has been described as dirty white or yellow in color. There is a long tail that has been described as looking like a thick fur covered whip. The arms are long and covered with the same fur that covers the rest of its body. The hands have long jagged fingers with long sharp claws. The head is also covered with dirty white and yellow fur. The top of the head appears to have large thick horns that resemble what you would see on a large ram. The eyes are black as coal and large teeth protruding for its mouth. The creature has a vocal scream that is guttural and can be heard for miles.

Some eyewitnesses claim they have seen the creature in the distance carrying what looked like to be a large deer. Another witness was hunting when he heard a loud cracking noise. Upon investigation, the hunter described seeing a Sheep-squatch slamming the horns on its head on the side of a large tree. The creature noticed the hunter and let out a gut-wrenching howl. The hunter fled the location in fear of being attacked. There are still to this day sightings of this creature throughout the northeastern side of the state.

———

IN BOTETOURT COUNTY there is a Bigfoot that stands seven-feet-tall and has been witnessed near the James River area in 2000. A couple were hiking in the area and enjoying the tranquility of the forest. There are a few small trails that lead through the wooded area. They left the trails and ventured deeper into the forest. This was an area they knew well, so they were not concerned about getting lost but set their GPS coordinates so they could be led back to the trail if needed. As they moved through the thick area of tree's, one of the hikers noticed movement in the distance. He pointed the area out to the other hiker. They stopped and just watched as the figure went back and forth. It was dark in color and was without a doubt standing straight up. At first, they thought it is possibly a person in a ghillie suit, but the figure seemed to make a grunting kind of snarling noise which would seem strange for someone to do. They moved in a little closer but still could not make out exactly what it was.

For no apparent reason, the figure took off running with loud thumps and disappeared. The hikers waited a few moments then went over to the area. They found large broken logs laying on the ground. They also noticed what appeared to be a footprint in the soil. It was twice the size of the man's foot who wore a size twelve. They left the area after a few moments and continued their hike. They still hike the area, but now spend their time searching for the creature.

48

King County, WA
WEST COAST BIGFOOT

WASHINGTON, whose capital is Olympia, was granted its statehood in 1889, and was the 42nd state to join the union. The state was named in honor of "George Washington," and is the only state in the US to be named after a president. Washington has an approximate population of 6.9 million residents, while covering an area of 71,298 square miles. In 1980, Mount Saint Helens erupted and was the deadliest, most economically destructive volcanic event in US history. The state is known to some as the "Evergreen State," and is the nation's leading producer of apples, with over eleven billion apples harvested each year.

Washington is also known for the Sammamish tribe. The Sammamish people were hunters, farmers, and fisherman. The people would hunt and feast on fish, deer, elk, bear, and even smaller animals such as squirrels, and raccoons. They would also farm such foods as corn and squash. The men wore breech cloths, buckskin leggings, moccasins and a robe or blanket type of robe. They lived in shelters called a longhouse. The longhouses had wooden roofs with doors on both side of the shelter. There was also a "smoke hole" in the middle to allow light and air in. The wigwam shelter was cone shaped with a wooded frame which could easily be set up and taken down. Upon research of the tribe's lore, my search came up inconclusive with no real lore to report.

———

WASHINGTON STATE IS the West Coast epicenter for Sasquatch sightings, and encounters. The state holds the record for most sightings in the country which is approximately over six hundred. The first recorded sighting came from a letter written in 1840 by Rev. Elkanah Walker. The letter referenced native Americans speaking of a group of "giant people." The giants were described as covered with hair and would steal fish and other types of food from the people. If this reporting is correct, the hairy giant people have changed how they interact with humans and have had to become more stealth in their ways to survive and exist.

———

ON MAY 18, 1980, the state of Washington witnessed a historical event. It was the eruption. Mount Saint Helens. A volcano that blew half the mountain apart and the explosion left volcanic dust across the state, and even into neighboring states. The significance of this information leads up to the first report of a flying humanoid creature in the area. It is believed that the creature was released when the volcano erupted. This such creature is known today as the Batsquatch. This flying anomaly is described by eyewitnesses as resembling a large gorilla with huge bat-like wings. Many of the sightings in the 80s were confined to the Mount Saint Helens area. The sightings of the beast made local and national news, which increased researcher attendance in the state. As time passed, there seemed to be missing pets and livestock. The Batsquatch is considered the main suspect in some of these strange occurrences involving missing pets and farm animals. Some believe the Batsquatch could also be involved in some human disappearances. Many believe the creature hunts down and captures its prey, and then flies back to the area of Mount Saint Helens, where most believe the creature dwells. To this day locals still claim the creature exists, and says it still makes an appearance in the local area.

IN KING COUNTY in the early 1980s, a couple of friends were on ATV's near Rattlesnake Lake, just outside of North Bend. As they were coming back from the end of their ride they came to an area where they saw in the distance a possible hunter. It appeared to look like it was crouching behind a bush. They figured the person was going to the bathroom. As they approached the figure stood up. It certainly was not a hunter or a person. Without a doubt, it was a Bigfoot. They sped on by the figure, and as they passed it turned and retreated into the woods making huge strides with its long legs. They did not stop until they were well out of the area. They pulled over in shock. They could not believe what they had witnessed. They describe the beast as being in the eight-foot-tall range, with no neck, wide shoulders, long legs and covered with black hair. Later that day, the two went back to the area in a truck to look for tracks, and other possible evidence. They came up empty.

49

Summers County, WV
HUMANOID CREATURE

WEST VIRGINIA, whose statehood was granted in 1863, was the 35th state to join the union. The state's population is approximately 1.9 million, while covering an area of 24,230 square miles. When the state of Virginia voted to secede from the United States during the Civil War (1861-1865), the people of the rugged and mountainous western region of the state opposed the decision and organized to form their own state. West Virginia is a major coal-producing state supplying over fifteen percent of the United States coal. The New River Gorge Bridge near Fayetteville is the longest steel arch bridge in the world. Every October, the town hosts a Bridge Day celebration when the road is closed to traffic, and individuals can parachute and bungee jump off the bridge. The event attracts close to 100,000 participants and spectators each year.

The Conoy Indians related to the Delaware tribe, did not move a lot like most other tribes. The men were the hunters and fisherman of the tribe, while the women cooked and cleaned while caring for the children. The Conoy diet would consist of fish, wild turkey, and deer. Corn was also another important part of their diet. They were known to have common weapons for fighting and hunting such as bow and arrow, spears, tomahawks, and clubs. The women wore wrap-around skirts with deerskin type shawls. The men wore leather leggings, breechcloths, with buckskin shirts. The tribe's people were known for their woodcarvings and artistic pottery. The tribes people spoke of a large creature that would roam the land. It is said to be of a spirit form but could become earthly and abduct women and children if they wandered away from the village.

NO DOUBT if one is into creatures and folklore, your already familiar with the Mothman. First spotted in 1966 by some gravediggers, it's blamed for the collapse of the Silver Bridge in Point Pleasant. It is said that wherever the Mothman is seen, disaster is sure to follow. There was a witness that claimed they saw it sitting on top of the bridge prior to its collapse. It is reported, as a long winged man-size creature with red glowing eyes. It is said that if you look into the eyes it can easily over-take you putting you in a trans-like state.

There was another sighting by a couple in a car who claim the winged creature chased them as they drove down the road. They stated as the car picked up speed, the creature kept up with ease flying beside the automobile and hovering over the top. The owner of the car described deep claw marks on the roof of the car, believing the Mothman to be the cause. There are rumors that it is still roaming the area. Each year, the town of Point Pleasant, West Virginia holds a festival in honor of the legend.

IN SUMMERS COUNTY, there does not seem to be any Mothman reports, but you can certainly find reports of Bigfoot encounters such as the one that took place in the Bluestone Lake area, just outside of the town of Hinton. A man was walking down a mountain when he came across a creature in a creek bed. The creature was described as over seven-feet-tall and could possibly weigh up to six-hundred-pounds. The arms were described as extremely long and covered with dark brown fur. The face was also described as very "ape-like." The witness described the beast as a "large humanoid" creature, which walked standing up but was a little hunched over. The creature made eye contact with the man, but quickly retreated into the woods. The man said he was no more than 30 yards away from the creature, so there is no doubt in his mind of what he saw that day.

50

Clark County, WI
WISCONSIN EYE SHINE

WISCONSIN, the 30th state to join the union, was granted its statehood in 1848. The states capital is Madison and has an approximate population of 5.8 million. The state covers an area of 65,496 square miles. Wisconsin became a US Territory following the American Revolution. The state attracted many settlers looking for work in lumber, dairy, and mining. Wisconsin leads the nation in dairy production especially in the area of cheese. Some residents of the state refer to each other as "cheese heads."

Also, from Wisconsin you will hear of the Chippewa tribe. Like other tribes the men did the hunting, and the women did the cooking and cleaning. Both the men and women did the farming to harvest food. The tribe was known for its artwork and music. The Chippewa lived in village's made of birchbark houses called wigwams. The women wore long dresses, that usually consisted of removable sleeves. On their feet they wore moccasins. The men wore the traditional breechcloths, with leggings. The men's hair was a shaved head, which was described as a "Mohawk" style, while the women had long hair which was usually braided. The Chippewa people spoke of a panther type water creature. Said to live in a body of water that the tribe would frequent. It is said the panthers' tail would rise out of the water and knock boats over or pull swimmers into the water to drown them. According to the witnesses, the tail was made of metal and could be used to sink a boat.

━━━

NO DOUBT if one has investigated creatures and beasts in the state, they would hear of "The Beast of Bray Road." It is also referred to as the "Wisconsin Werewolf." Originally, the beast was spotted in Elkhorn in 1936, but it is said to now be moving all through the state. Some witnesses have described it as "humanoid," with canine features. Others believe the creature to have a bear-like body but with a wolf-like head. Many encounters have taken place on Bray Road. One encountered was described as seeing a large wolf running through a field on the side of the roadway. The witness was surprised at the agility and speed the of the animal and impressed that it could keep up with the car. The next event that took place defies all-natural ability of a four-legged animal. Without missing a beat, the animal stood up on its hind-legs and continued to run alongside the car. The creature then turned, dropped down on all fours and disappeared into a think bushy area. Like many other states who have witnessed "werewolf" type creatures, some say it is a Bigfoot that has been misidentified. The locals in the area of Bray Road disagree.

━━━

A COUPLE of young boys in Clark County according to their parents, witnessed what they believe to be a Bigfoot without any concerns of a misidentification. In 2012 in the later evening hours of a summer evening, two brothers were out on their back porch. They started doing howl calls, this is what Bigfoot researchers perform while out in the woods. As they did, a short time later, they heard movement in a wooded area in their back yard. As they stared in the direction of the noise, they saw what they described as a set of glowing eyes, or eye shine. The area where the eyes appeared were in the seven-foot range. They said they tried another howl to see if they could get the eyes to move. The eyes just remained and stared back. A few moments later they saw them darken and disappear. When they vanished, they could hear some movement in the wooded area.

They ran inside to tell their parents that they had just seen a Bigfoot. The next morning when it was light out, they surveyed the area for possible signs with their father and found what could be the imprint of a large foot but was not enough to confirm. The dad believes what they saw was an owl in a tree. The boys disagree, and truly believe what they were looking at was in fact, a Bigfoot.

51

Washakie County, WY
SHOTGUN SASQUATCH

WYOMING, also known as the "Equality State," was the 44th state to join the union in 1890. The states capital is Cheyenne and has an approximate population of five hundred and eighty-thousand residents while covering an area of 97,812 square miles. In 1920, Wyoming was the first state to allow women to vote, which was a huge achievement and is recognized as one of the victories of the American Women's movement. The state is the 10th largest in the country but even with its size has one of the smallest populations. When in the state, you can visit the famous "Yellowstone National Park," and also visit "Old Faithful," one of the largest hot springs in the country. Wyoming also has many museums such as "The Buffalo Bill Center of the West" in Cody, "The National Museum of Wildlife Art" in Jackson and "The Wyoming State Museum."

The Shoshone Indians have lived in Wyoming since the seventeenth century. The people lived in teepees made from hunted buffalo skins. The teepees were easily set up and taken down which was ideal when having to move from location to location. As expert buffalo hunters, the buffalo can provide the tribe with all they need for shelter, clothing, and nutrition.

Originally the people were both hunters and farmers, but once they acquired horses, they for the most part gave up farming to follow the seasonal migrations of the buffalo herds. The most common weapon was the bow and arrow. The people were known for their skill for shooting arrows. The Shoshone also used spears and shields. They are known to hunt deer and elk and consume plants and wild berries. The Shoshone people did all they could to avoid the "Nimerigar." A furious and violent troll-like group of little people. Said to have magical powers with a thirst and hunger for human flesh. Many unexplained deaths and attacks were believed to have been the doing of this evil race of people.

───

IN WYOMING, there is a legend of the "De Smet Lake Monster." Like most it is described by some as a snake-like serpent around forty-feet-long, and as big around as a tree. Others in the area have given details of the creature appearing to be alligator-like. Floating on the surface of the water, then slowly sinking down to the depths of the murky water. One characteristic of the creature that remains the same from witness to witness, is its head is described as very "horse-like" in shape. This description is also very similar to witnesses of Champ, the Lake Champlain Monster.

There are stories of this creature dating back decades, stating the creature to be aggressive in nature and many Native Americans fell victim to the beast while bathing and fishing. Other victims fell prey while on the banks of the water while others in boats found themselves flipped upside down struggling to get to land. In many cases, not everyone escaped the creatures attack, and those who did not, were never seen again. The beast has been said to lunge at individuals who are close to the water very much in the way an alligator does. The De Smet

Lake Monster is said to still dwell in the murky depths of the lake, patiently awaiting its next victim.

⸻

IF EVER IN the state and traveling on Route 90 near the town of Saddlestring, stop and visit the lake. You might just get a glimpse of the creature. In 2005 in Washakie County, a farmer made a report about a strange creature spooking his cows. It was in the early morning hours and still quite dark outside. The farmer was out tending to his herd of cattle. In the distance he could see some of them acting strange, and all running in the same direction away from a certain area in the field. Believing a predator of some kind was responsible for the commotion the farmer ran, got his shot gun, and ran out to the area to see what was spooking his cattle. When he arrived at the edge of the field near the corner of a fence post, he could not believe what he was seeing.

It was an upright monster. It was described as eight-feet-tall, possibly having brown fur, and in the six-hundred-pound range. It turned, looked at the farmer and started moving toward him. The farmer in a panic shot his rifle. The creature stopped, then retreated, and disappeared into the darkness. All that remained was the upset cattle making noises and gathering into a huddle in the opposite corner of the field. Once the sun appeared, the farmer investigated where he saw the creature stop and turn to look for evidence. There was no sign of blood or fur in the area. He did come across what he believed to be footprints in some soft wet ground but did not take pictures. No other encounters or sightings have taken place on his property since.

Afterword

Monsters, could they be real? Could they exist in a world that is mostly inhabited by humans and still survive? From Bigfoot, to Champ in the waters of Lake Champlain, one would believe with all the witnesses from the beginning of recorded history, there must be something extremely real too this phenomenon. It has been said, that one who has monsters on their brain, will see what they want to see. I challenge that way of thinking, and believe in the future as science progresses, a lot of the questions we have today, will be answered. Whether we will like the answers or not, until that day presents itself, keep your eyes and ears open. Always know what is behind you and continue the search.

Bibliography

- *Accessgenealogy (2020)*
- *All About History*, (2002-2018)
- Bailey, Col, *Shadow of the Thylacine* (Mike Press 2013)
- Bartholomew, Paul & Robert, Brann, William Hallenbeck.
- *Monsters of the Northwoods.* Utica NY North Country Books (1992)
- Coleman, Loren, Mysterious America (Faber & Faber 1983)
- Department of History, *Front E-history* (2018-2019)
- Education Commission of the States (2018-2019)
- Fact Monster (2000-2019)
- Freeman, Richard, *Adventures in Crypto zoology* (mango,2019)
- Godfrey, Linda, *American Monsters*, Penguin, (2014)
- History, *Famous Inventors*, ThoughtCo (201)9
- Holiday, FW, *The Great Orm of Loch Ness* (Faber & Faber, 1968)
- Landsburg, Alan, *In Search of Myths and Monsters* (Corgi, 1977)

- Native American History (2017-2019)
- Native American History, *Changing the Narrative*, The Great Course Daily (2019 updated)
- *Native American, Indigenous People*, Encyclopedia Britannica (2000 to 2019)
- *Overview Native Americans*, Scholastic (2016)
- Office of the Historian, US Department of State (2019)
- *Rock on the Net*, (1997 to 2019)
- *Scientific American*, (2017)
- Sykes, Bryan, *Nature of the Beast* (Coronet, 2015)
- US States, *Info Please* (2019)
- Some cases not specific enough to reference

About the Author

Kenney W. Irish AKA "The Cryptopunkologist," is an author, hardcore/punk musician and sales/marketing profession-al. Originally from the northern parts of Vermont, he recently re-located to the beautiful Adirondacks area of upstate New York. He's had a love of folklore, legends, monsters, and U.F.O stories his entire life and turned that passion into books, speaking engagements, television and co-hosting a radio show. For more information visit him at www.kwirish.com

f facebook.com/kenney.irish.1

🐦 twitter.com/Kirisheae

📷 instagram.com/kenneyirishauthor

Made in the USA
Middletown, DE
05 February 2023